TIMOTHY
THE TORTOISE

TIMOTHY THE TORTOISE

The Remarkable Story of the Nation's Oldest Pet

RORY KNIGHT BRUCE

ORION

First published in hardback in Great Britain in 2004
by Orion Books
an imprint of the Orion Publishing Group Ltd
Orion House, 5 Upper St Martin's Lane,
London WC2H 9EA

A CIP catalogue record for this book is available from the British Library.

ISBN 0752868721

Printed and bound in Great Britain by
Butler and Tanner Ltd, Frome and London

www.orionbooks.co.uk

'I am he that is. I am the world itself, come to pay you a visit. In another sense I am an outcast – almost an outlaw. If you prefer a less materialistic view, I am a sort of fate – the retribution that waits its time.'

Joseph Conrad, *Victory*

Contents

Illustrations

Foreword

When Timothy the Tortoise died at Powderham Castle in Devon in the spring of 2004, it was estimated that he was more than 160 years old. This great span, giving him a birth date some time around 1844, made him the oldest living resident in England.

In May 1998, I interviewed Timothy for the first time. He responded well to my enquiries, published in the *Daily Telegraph*, and proved himself to be every bit the enthusiastic subject I had known since my childhood.

Against the stricture of his label – 'My name is Timothy. I am very old. Please do not pick me up' – I was allowed to hold him, feed him on lettuce leaves and encourage him to those feats of movement which only a chelonian in advanced years knows. His wise look, the leather upon his neck like a worn dog chew, the patina of light upon his carapace, will remain with me for ever. He appeared as an innocent being in a changing world.

His good fortune was to fall into the hands of the Courtenay family, his custodians for more than a century. As Earls of Devon, their seat has been at Powderham for more than 600 years and they have been in the county since the early Middle Ages. As befits the more enlightened members of the English aristocracy, they knew their place, and Timothy knew his.

Powderham is one of the oldest family houses in England. Its sixty rooms include a Dining Hall, State

Bedroom, Gold Drawing Room, Music Room, unique eighteenth-century library bookcases and a grand staircase forming part of the medieval castle. In the Dining Room there is a narwhal or whale's horn, listed as a unicorn's horn, once used to detect poison in food or drink by changing colour.

The Powderham estate, which stretches along the estuary of the River Exe, is fertile, mild in climate, and one of the most beautiful in Devon. It was founded not on the fortunes of the Industrial Revolution but by earlier royal patronage, warfare and some good old-fashioned pillaging in the thirteenth and fourteenth centuries. Today, agriculture is still one of the most important activities of the estate. But its opening to the public in 1960 reflected the need of many large houses in the post-war years, to diversify, or fail.

Among the many schemes for survival was one of the earliest 'car boot' or attic sales in 1965, conducted by the redoubtable 17th Countess of Devon. Included were several stuffed birds, a Regency bedpan, a battered telescope and an imitation-brass bamboo tripod once used for making tea in the Rose Garden where Timothy lived. 'I am delighted to say,' commented Venetia Devon at the time, 'there will be fewer things to dust.'

On another occasion, in 1972, the Devons invited ex-miner Harry Seymour and fifty Geordie pitmen for a day of whippet racing. 'It will enable the lads to get out and see how the other half lives,' Seymour told the *Northern Daily Mail*. This was not thought to have been a money-spinner for the estate.

How the 'other half' were living at Powderham until very recently was under the cloud of post-war austerity. In

1983, the Devons took the step of advertising the castle for rent, planning to move into a cottage. On offer were thirty bedrooms, eight bathrooms and the historic courtyard, for £800 a week. There were no takers. As the Earl of Devon's son, Lord Courtenay, said at the time: 'It costs more than £50,000 a year to run the castle and gardens. Even in a good year we lose £15,000.'

But Powderham, like Timothy, has been a great survivor, and there have been strokes of luck. In 1988, the Victoria & Albert Museum and the National Art Collections Fund paid £455,000 for the two twelve-foot bookcases at Powderham, built in 1740 by Exeter cabinet-maker John Channon. They broke the record for the most expensive pieces of English furniture sold in Britain. The sale attracted howls of protest as the bookcases, and therefore the family, were allowed to remain in the castle.

Timothy was never allowed indoors, resting, as he did often, among the safe girdle of the Powderham Rose Garden. That he endured the reign of six monarchs, and saw out the lives of seven Earls of Devon, marks his place in the natural history of the world.

During the Second World War, Timothy created his own air-raid shelter at Powderham to avoid the bombs that nightly rained on Exeter. Even a German bomber which strafed and killed a walking farmhand passed him by.

In winter, he made his own hibernation spot under the giant wisteria, using its discarded leaves. He endured the frozen winters of 1947 and 1963, in which the West Country came to an icy and snow-blown standstill.

The quiet courage of Timothy's life captured the world's

imagination at his death. But it is to the Earl of Devon and Countess of Devon, and to Eric Bailey, my then editor at the *Daily Telegraph*, that I owe my gratitude. Without them, my literary agent John Beaton and Ian Marshall, publishing director at Orion, the life of Timothy the Tortoise might have lain forever undisturbed at the bottom of the garden.

Rory Knight Bruce
Devon
July 2004

Introduction

News of Timothy's death was reported around the world. He captured the popular imagination as much for his longevity as for his experience. Somewhere between melancholy and courage, his life was at once simple but all seeing. If there is to be a word for wisdom in old age, let it now be *timothesis*.

Timothy, so named after Gilbert White's eighteenth-century tortoise, who lived in the walled garden at Selborne in Hampshire, had a career as varied and brave as his character.

He was born in Turkey and was of the species *Testudo græca*, once common on the shores of the Mediterranean. As a species, he was also referred to as *Testudo græca Linnæus*, after Carl Linnaeus, the eighteenth-century Swedish taxonomist who classified the spur-thighed tortoise in 1758. The Greeks called them *oepeoikoi* or 'house-carriers'.

In 1926, the 14th Earl of Devon, 'Uncle Charlie', a member of the Zoological Society of London, decided to take Timothy there to be mated (chelonian dynasties being as important as aristocratic ones). It was discovered that Timothy was really a Timothea. All members of the family steadfastly refused to accept this and he remained Timothy to the end.

He had, to those, like myself, who were allowed to pick him up, the calming density and weight of a medium-sized Le Creuset pot. He was, when last weighed, in 1995,

4.08 kilogrammes (9 pounds).

It is thought that Timothy was born in Turkish Mediterranean waters in about 1844, although he may even have been born before that. Much of his earlier life was spent as a ship's mascot, seeing service with his owner Captain John Guy Courtenay-Evered, RN, on HMS *Queen* at the first bombardment of the Siege of Sebastopol in 1854. 'This entitled him to the Crimean Service Medal (1854–6) with Sebastopol bar,' says the naval historian Captain Guy Crowden, RN (retired). 'It was a sign of his modesty that he chose not to wear it.'

(Although the time for claiming campaign medals had passed, one sailor successfully did so from the Siege of Sebastopol, forty-seven years after he had been on board. When struck, the medal on its lower part read 'baby', as he had been born on board during the bombardment.)

John Guy Courtenay-Evered was from the cadet or junior branch of the Courtenay family, of which there are thousands living all over the world. In 1904, he changed his name to Courtenay-Everard, before dying at the age of 100 in 1931. He also saw service in the East Indies and China on the HMS *Princess Charlotte* and the HMS *Nankin*. Shortly after his death *The Times* published an account of his remarkable life called *A Centenarian's Memories*.

The Courtenays of Powderham are an ancient Frankish family whose pennon waved on the battlefields of Crecy and Agincourt. They came to England in the time of Henry II.

In the thirteenth century, the family provided three Latin Emperors of Constantinople, beginning a history of religious duty that has endured to the present day. A

Courtenay was among the founding Knights of the Garter and their earldom of Devon and residence at Powderham date to the early fourteenth century.

William Courtenay was Archbishop of Canterbury from 1382 until his death in 1396. He is buried in Canterbury Cathedral at the feet of the Black Prince. The 9th Earl and 3rd Viscount, renowned as one of the most beautiful boys in eighteenth-century England, attracted the amorous attention of William Beckford of Fonthill in Wiltshire, a man of unbridled gothic tastes and licentiousness. Because of this he also attracted the soubriquet 'Kitty' Courtenay.

There have been plenty of other members, some triumphant, some tragic, over the years. Two were lost on the SS *Titanic*, another went up in flames when her balldress caught light from a candle. Several have disappeared on ships, never to be seen again, and one, Thomas Courtenay, who was a Privy Councillor to George IV and MP for Totnes, drowned while bathing off Torquay in 1841.

The 12th Earl was simply called 'Naughty Baldwin'. Although he was an MP and Deputy Lieutenant of Devon, he never married. 'He had plenty of children but none of them with benefit of clergy,' says Lady Katherine Watney, sister of the present, 18th Earl of Devon.

By the time he was thirty-five, Naughty Baldwin was bankrupt to the tune of £8,000. From the late A.B. Rowland's *Historic Notes on Notable Courtenays AD 1000–2000*, we learn: 'There is evidence that he recognised and provided for at least some of these illicit families, though they were forbidden to meet or make themselves known to members of his family.'

'*Ubi lapsus, quid feci*' is the Courtenay family motto,

created in the sixteenth century. 'Where have I fallen, what have I done?' Edward Gibbon, in his *Decline and Fall*, calls it 'the plaintive motto which asserts the innocence, and deplores the fall, of this ancient house'. The answer in Timothy's case is that he did quite a lot before falling into safe and caring hands. And it is true to say that, like their beloved chelonian, the family have kept their heads down for the past couple of hundred years.

In 1892, Timothy passed from Courtenay-Everard to a midshipman, Edward Rutherfoord, who later rose to captain's rank. It was said among the family that Courtenay-Everard's next port of call was to be Antarctica, and that Timothy jumped ship at Portsmouth.

Edward Rutherfoord gave him to his brother, Thomas, who married Harriette Corrie of the Elms, Itchen Abbas, in Hampshire. From them, Timothy went to Harriette's sister Mary, who married John Silva, also of Itchen Abbas. She was the great-grandmother of the present Earl of Devon.

Members of all three families – Corries, Rutherfoords and Silvas – may be found buried in the pretty church of St John the Baptist in Itchen Abbas. It was rebuilt in 1862 on the site of a Norman church first constructed there in 1092.

The Silvas were noted Portuguese nobles and importers of port and sherry. John Silva's grandfather, Bruno Everisto Ferara da Silva, was the son of a canon and a Portuguese princess. This has, in some accounts, given rise to the notion that Timothy was once mascot to a Portuguese man-o'-war.

'I think there was some dark history to him,' says Lady Gabrielle Courtenay of Bruno da Silva. At ninety-one

Gabrielle (pronounced 'Gabriel') is John and Mary Silva's granddaughter and the person who has known Timothy the longest. 'But I don't think he was a pirate or anything like that.'

From Charles Sellers' *Oporto Old and New*, published in 1899, there is an account of Bruno da Silva.

> In the early part of the nineteenth century, when we were nearly always at war with France, Mr Bruno Silva considered it advisable for the safety of his property, to equip a privateer of nine guns. In this ship, cargoes of wine were consigned to him, the basis being thus laid of a business destined to become one of the most important in the port wine trade.
>
> It does not require any very great stretch of the imagination to credit this nine-gun privateer with having had to show her teeth on various occasions to the warships of *la grande nation*, and it is just as probable that at other times she has owed her safety to showing a clean pair of heels.
>
> It is creditable to our countrywomen to record that Mr Bruno Silva married an English lady, and took up residence in England for good. By many years of residence he acquired all the rights and privileges of an Englishman, although to the last he was not able to thoroughly master the language of his adopted country.

Lady Gabrielle's earliest memories of Timothy were as a child at the Honiton Rectory where her father, Frederick Leslie Courtenay, the third son of the 13th Earl of Devon, was the vicar. The 13th Earl, also a vicar, had married Anna Maria Leslie, daughter of the Countess of Rothes, whose family motto is 'Grip fast'. Timothy certainly did that.

'He was about the size of a hassock,' says Lady Gabrielle. 'He just appeared one day in a wicker basket towards the end of the Great War.' From that time, until Timothy's death, they were never parted, as Lady Gabrielle moved to Powderham with him and her parents in 1935, and then to live near by.

At first, from the early 1920s, Timothy would travel by train from Honiton to the station at Starcross near Powderham for family holidays. The family still had the right to stop any train there, a privilege last used in 1966, when Lady Katherine Courtenay married Antony Watney.

Much of Timothy's good fortune, health and long life may be put down to the fact that Powderham, and in particular the Rose Garden and ancient wisteria under which he lived on the lawn, is a microclimate of mild weather. He was also tended by family, gardeners and, later, staff who showed visitors round the castle after it was opened to the public in 1960.

Timothy became something of an affectionate attraction, although it is true to say that before I undertook my interview with him in 1998, he had lain undisturbed with his diet of dandelion leaves, strawberries and lettuce. No one undertaking a serious investigation of this ancient being could fail to be struck by his character, his gimlet eye of kindness, and his movement. 'He could certainly get a lick on when he wanted to,' recalls Lady Katherine Watney.

He didn't mind visitors, nor the distractions of Merchant Ivory filming Kazuo Ishiguro's *The Remains of the Day* all around him in 1993. The film starred Emma Thompson, Sir Anthony Hopkins, Hugh Grant, Edward Fox and Christopher Reeve. Only Christopher Reeve is believed to have met him.

When concert performers also started coming to Powderham at this time, Timothy was to hand when drinks were served to Chris de Burgh, Steve Harley, Rick Parfitt of Status Quo, Dame Kiri Te Kanawa and Roger Daltrey of The Who. Timothy certainly didn't hope he would die before he got old.

Tim Miles, who looked after the Rose Garden for six years until 1984, remembers Timothy with great fondness.

> I worked a lot in the Rose Garden under the watchful eye of Timothy. I had a special affection for Timothy, as that is also my name. He used to follow me around the garden as I was weeding and dead-heading the roses. I think that this was mainly due to the fact that I used to feed him with rose petals. Sometimes, if I was particularly busy and did not give him his petals, he would come and remind me by ramming into me with his shell. In the summer on bare ankles it was occasionally a little painful but I always got the message.
>
> I am sure that you are aware of his passion for strawberries and ladies' toenails that had red nail polish on them. I have had to rescue several damsels in distress when they have been chased around the garden by a rather single-minded tortoise.
>
> I was never allowed to tidy up under the large wisteria that grows up the side of the castle as that was where Timothy hibernated. I always looked forward to seeing him in the spring when he first emerged from his slumbers. Once or twice I had to turn him up the right way after he had slithered down the bank into what was then an herbaceous border.

He was a fearless little chap and a real character. He knew that he was the boss in the garden and would never move out of the way when I was cutting the grass, always taking his own time.

I was very sad when I heard that he had died as I had spent so much time with just him for company in the garden. I am very pleased to hear that his memory will live on in your book.

Timothy also had a companion tortoise in the Rose Garden called Toby, who lived to be about sixty. 'Sadly, I had to bury Toby in 1984,' says Tim Miles. 'I am not sure if it was coincidence but my successor as gardener was called Toby.'

Lady Katherine Watney also remembers having to turn Timothy the right way up when he fell on to his back by the garden parapet in an attempt to descend the stone stairs leading down to the lower lake. 'We kept chickens there during the war and he clearly wanted to know what the fuss was about,' says Lady Katherine.

Powderham today, with its sixty rooms, deer park, sawmill and gardens overlooking the estuary towards Exmouth and Topsham, is an oasis of calm on a busy Devon coastline. The main London railway line, built by Isambard Kingdom Brunel, hugs the coast near by, giving its passengers a view of where Timothy lived out his life as a landlubber.

Above, on the highest point of the 3,500-acre estate, a ruined belvedere, once the home of the head keeper before the last war, until he developed appendicitis and it fell into ruin, looks out across the river. To the north is Exeter and the Exeter Ship Canal, to the right the

River Clyst where it joins the Exe. Over the river, the white Royal Marine base at Lympstone stands out near a low yellow house, Nutwell Court, once home to Sir Francis Drake, whose widow married into the Courtenay family.

It was not just the newspapers which reported Timothy's death. He became the subject of a quiz question on the television programme *Have I Got News for You*, and was featured on the BBC's *Jonathan Ross* radio programme. *Private Eye* undertook a gentle parody of Lord (Bill) Deedes, the former Tory minister and *Daily Telegraph* editor, still reporting for the paper at ninety-one. 'Bill the Tortoise – Not Dead' ran the headline.

> The world's oldest surviving tortoise, Old Bill, was reported to be alive and well and working for the *Daily Telegraph*. For the last 160 years, Bill has been sitting in a corner, living on scraps of news, and occasionally coming out of his shell to go to Ethiopia or India.
>
> The World that Bill the Tortoise has seen:
>
> - Noah's Ark. Bill was one of the first on board.
> - Magna Carta. Bill was under the famous table at Runnymede.
> - Repeal of the Corn Laws. Bill was in the House of Lords, sitting underneath the Woolsack.
> - Sinking of the *Titanic*. Bill had to swim all the way home.

Jeremy Clarkson, the foremost British writer and presenter on speed, slowed down to consider Timothy in an article. He attributed Timothy's long life to the fact that he did not go jogging, cycling or playing squash, play tennis or go mountain biking. 'His idea of rambling was a stroll to the lettuce patch for lunch,' wrote Clarkson. 'So there you are. If you want to live long and prosper, sit around a lot and make no sudden movements.'

In all parody there is truth, and the truth is that in Timothy's 160 years, with his all-seeing eye, he witnessed a greater span of history than any human ever could. I have been asked how I could write about him when he spent half of the year asleep. But the subject of every biography is asleep for a third of his or her life.

Some years ago, Timothy was submitted by the family for inclusion in the *Guinness Book of Records*, but the submission was not successful. The adjudicators were not satisfied as to his age and required a birth certificate. There are, however, plans under consideration that the noun timothesis should be included in the *Oxford English Dictionary*. The meaning would be 'wisdom in old age'.

Technically, as *Testudo græca*, Timothy is a reptile. But somehow the word seems too harsh to be included in this history of his life, in which he saw so much and said so little – although among the e-mails of condolence posted on the website after his death is one from Canada, which reads: 'Our thoughts are with you. Bless you, dear departed reptile.'

He was born in the age of Queen Victoria, and outlasted six monarchs. When the late Lord Devon died in 1998, the *Daily Telegraph* carried the news on its front page, illustrated with a photograph of Timothy, to soften the blow. 'With the death of the 17th Earl of Devon, another generation has passed at Powderham, but its oldest inhabitant remains unperturbed. Insulated by a deep bed of wisteria leaves, Timothy the Tortoise sleeps on.' With Timothy's death, the blows may no longer be softened.

I have only ever once seen a *Testudo græca* in the wild. Walking several miles to have lunch one day in 1998 with Patrick Leigh-Fermor in the Greek Peloponnese, I entered a gorge by Old Kardamyli. The white-bouldered riverbed was empty of water. I walked its course past an old monastery, deep below the small chapel of St Nicholas where travel writer Bruce Chatwin's ashes are buried beneath an olive tree in an unmarked grave.

In the hall and shade of that great ravine, there was a tortoise. It was like being face to face with another time, another empire. I was so surprised to stumble upon him that I watched the slow, certain movements of his claws, the head, unthreatened, beyond the reach of eagles, swiring in wonderment. I understood then why the Romans called the slow, sure movement of their 100 soldiers with shields a carapace or tortoise shell.

I had intended to begin this book with another quotation from Joseph Conrad, who, like Timothy, spent his youth on ships before settling into the English countryside, orphaned and far from his native land. In *Victory* the hero, Axel Heyst, is urged by his father: 'Look on – speak no sound.' But somehow, as I wrote and journeyed each day to Powderham a great weight was lifted from me. Like Gilbert White, I had succumbed to the enormity of his years, the sheer open arms of age and character. I had become, like Timothy, a sort of fate, the retribution that waits its time.

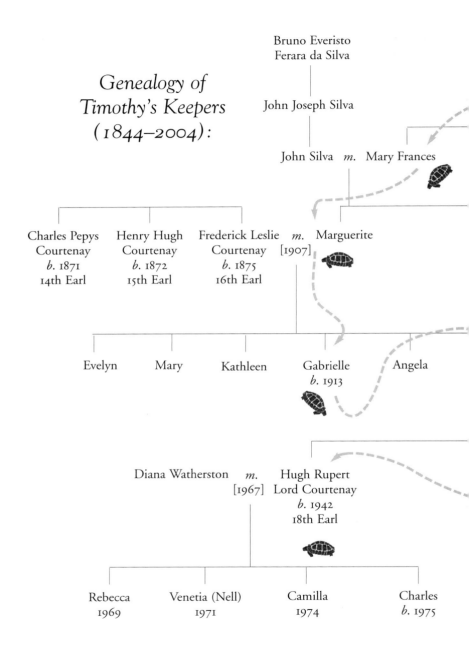

Genealogy of Timothy's Keepers (1844–2004):

Bruno Everisto
Ferara da Silva

John Joseph Silva

John Silva *m.* Mary Frances

Charles Pepys Courtenay
b. 1871
14th Earl

Henry Hugh Courtenay
b. 1872
15th Earl

Frederick Leslie Courtenay
b. 1875
16th Earl

m. [1907]

Marguerite

Evelyn

Mary

Kathleen

Gabrielle
b. 1913

Angela

Diana Watherston *m.* [1967] Hugh Rupert Lord Courtenay
b. 1942
18th Earl

Rebecca
1969

Venetia (Nell)
1971

Camilla
1974

Charles
b. 1975

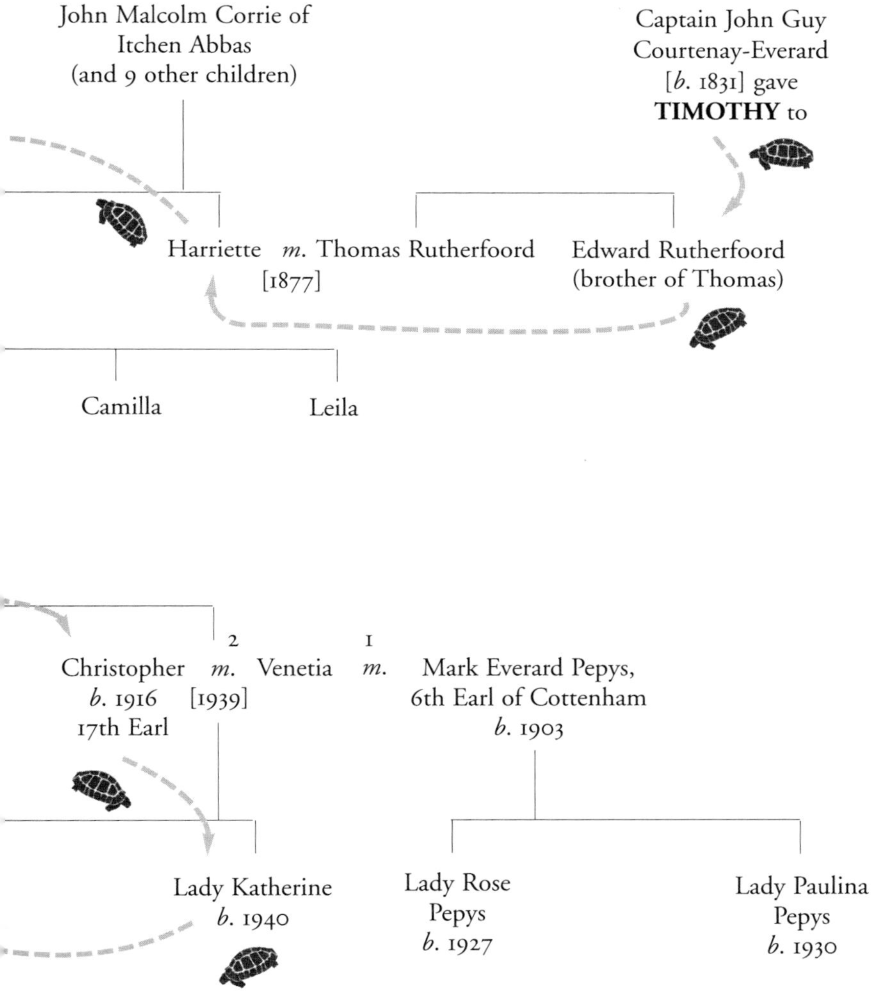

In 1935 Timothy moves permanently to Powderham

Timothy's Timeline

1844	Timothy born, *Testudo græca*, in the Mediterranean, probably on the Bosphorus.
1854	Timothy is a ship's mascot on the HMS *Queen* at the first bombardment of the Siege of Sebastopol. He is in the charge of Captain John Guy Courtenay-Everard.
1892	Timothy is given to Captain Edward Rutherfoord, Itchen Abbas, Hampshire.
1902	Timothy is given to Thomas and Harriette Rutherfoord (née Corrie).
1904	Timothy is given to John and Mary Silva (née Corrie).
1920	Timothy arrives at the Rectory, Honiton, home of the Reverend Frederick Courtenay and his wife Marguerite. He gets his own wooden hoop to stop him escaping.
1926	Timothy visits the Zoological Society of London with Charles, 14th Earl of Devon. He is found to be a Timothea.
1928	Timothy gets drunk on azalea blossom and receives a dose of castor oil from a silver spoon.
1942	Timothy makes his own bunker at Powderham Castle to avoid the bombing of Exeter.
1947	Powderham opens as a domestic science school.
1960	Powderham opens to the public.
1993	Powderham opens for pop concerts.
2004	Timothy dies.

One

The Selborne Tortoise

Timothy's famous forebear

> 'My greatest misfortune, and what I have never divulged to any one before, is the want of society of my own kind.'
>
> Letter from Gilbert White to 21-year-old Miss Hecky Mulso, written in the guise of his tortoise on 31 August 1784, headed 'from the border under the fruit wall' and signed 'Your Sorrowful Reptile'

No history of Timothy the Powderham Tortoise can be made without reference to Gilbert White's earlier tortoise of the same name. Gilbert White (1720–93), the eighteenth-century curate of Selborne in Hampshire was, like William Cobbett and the Reverend Francis Kilvert, the leading pastoral chronicler of his day.

In 1780, he inherited his tortoise Timothy from his widowed aunt, Mrs Rebecca Snooke, who lived at Ringmer in Sussex. The symbol of a tortoise is still used in the Sussex downland village today. We learn about the history and habits of the tortoise from Gilbert White's diaries and his *The Natural History and Antiquities of Selborne*. He had visited it in Sussex since 1770, when White was fifty, his aunt seventy-six and the tortoise guessed at being more than forty.

He was named Timothy the Tortoise not as a nickname but to distinguish him from a local farmer called Timothy Turner. At Powderham, staff would occasionally refer to the present general manager, Tim Faulkner, as 'Human Timothy'.

What arises in White's journals is the affection for the tortoise which crept up on him over the years. On 8 October 1770, White wrote to his regular correspondent, the Hon. Daines Barrington, about his chelonian discovery:

> A land tortoise, which has been kept for thirty years in a little walled garden belonging to the house where I am now visiting, retires under ground about the middle of *November*, and comes forth again about the middle of *April*. When it first appears in the spring it discovers very little inclination towards food; but in the height of summer grows voracious: and then as the summer declines its appetite declines; so that for the last six weeks in autumn it hardly eats at all. Milky plants, such as lettuces, dandelions, sowthistles, are its favourite dish. In a neighbouring village one was kept till by tradition it was supposed to be an hundred years old. An instance of vast longevity in such a poor reptile.

In the Rose Garden at Powderham, where Timothy enjoyed his own vast longevity, it may sometimes have surprised visitors that the lawns and borders were not kept in pristine condition. The answer is that these plants and lawns were Timothy's food.

The Rose Garden was a safe haven for Timothy. It is surrounded by the family chapel, the gothic arch of the front of the house and the library to the left. The State Bedroom, in which all Courtenay heirs are born, looks down on Timothy's place of hibernation.

On the fourth side, a low wall gives a view to the park and the Exe estuary beyond. It was both sunny and sheltered for Timothy, who hibernated under the purple-shooting Victorian wisteria. Its leaves, which he used as bedding, were never collected or disturbed. On the lawn, nourishing clover and dandelions were always allowed to grow.

Tim Miles, the gardener in charge of the Rose Garden from 1978 to 1984, recalls the layout. 'There were two herbaceous borders as well as the roses. These have now been replaced with more roses. As far as I am aware, Timothy only ever ate rose petals and dandelions (flowers and leaves).'

During that time Timothy's main diet was supplied by the 17th Earl and Countess of Devon. This, says Tim Miles, consisted mainly of strawberries, melon and lettuce. 'I never noticed any chunks out of the herbaceous plants but that does not mean he didn't have a little taste now and again.'

As for varying reports of Timothy's diet, Lady Katherine Watney is adamant: 'Timothy often ate strawberries when they were in season, but he never, as has been reported, ate strawberry leaves.'

On the outside walls are scramblers and climbers whose lower leaves and tendrils fell within his reach. It is valuable to record the full menu of roses available to Timothy:

Rosa 'Spanish Beauty'
Rosa 'Vicomtesse Pierre du Fou'

Rosa 'Pink Perpétué'
Rosa 'Adamis'
Rosa 'New Dawn'

All these were planted in the 1930s, which coincided with Timothy taking up full residence at the castle in 1935. Among the floribunda and tea roses, most of which are from the 1980s to 1990s, there are older roses such as 'Peace', 'Precious Platinum', 'Summer Fragrance', 'Sheila's Perfume', 'Freedom', 'Polar Star' and 'Champagne Cocktail'.

On the banks are ox-eye daisies, also known as marguerites. This is perhaps a coincidental family connection, as it was Marguerite, wife of Frederick Leslie, 16th Earl of Devon, who inherited Timothy from her mother Mary, daughter of John Malcolm Corrie of Itchen Abbas in Hampshire.

Marguerite Courtenay in the Rose Garden with Timothy in 1936.

The patient endeavours of the Ringmer tortoise are again observed by White in a letter to the Hon. Daines Barrington, dated 12 April 1772:

On the first of *November* I remarked that the old tortoise, formerly mentioned, began first to dig his hybernaculum, which it had fixed on just beside a great tuft of hepaticas. It scrapes out the ground with its fore-feet, and throws it up over its back with its hind; but the motion of its legs is ridiculously slow, little exceeding the hour-hand of a clock; and suitable to the composure of an animal said to be a whole month in performing one feat of copulation.

Nothing can be more assiduous than this creature night and day in scooping the earth, and forcing its great body into the cavity; but, as the noons of that season proved unusually warm and sunny, it was continually interrupted, and called forth by the heat in the middle of the day; and though I continued there till the thirteenth of *November*, yet the work remained unfinished.

No part of its behaviour ever struck me more than the extreme timidity it always expresses with regard to rain; for though it has a shell that would secure it against the wheel of a loaded cart, yet does it discover as much solicitude about rain as a lady dressed in all her best attire, shuffling away on the first sprinklings, and running its head up in a corner.

If attended to, it becomes an excellent weather glass; for as sure as it walks elate, and as it were on tiptoe, feeding with great earnestness in a morning, so sure will it rain before night.

The tortoise, like other reptiles, has an arbitrary stomach as well as lungs; and can refrain from eating as well as breathing for a great part of the year.

I was much taken with its sagacity in discerning those that do it kind offices; for as soon as the good old lady comes in sight who has waited on it for more than thirty years, it hobbles towards its benefactress with aukward alacrity; but remains inattentive to strangers. 'The ox knoweth his owner, and the ass his master's crib' (Isaiah 1:3).

'He would always come to my mother's call,' remembers Lady Gabrielle Courtenay of Powderham Timothy. And so it was with other members of the family who, like her, had a special care for him. 'He did not travel very far,' recalls Lady Rose Berger, eldest daughter of the 17th Countess of Devon. 'We did hear a story of him going down the front drive and having to be rescued, but I never saw that.'

Timothy was content to live in the Rose Garden. It restricted his movements, and so did he. Although there are tales of Timothy speeding across the lawn for food, or to bite a lady's varnished toenail, for the most part he was content to rise each day with one eye on the clock for bed-time.

In 1780, Mrs Snooke died, aged eighty-six, and Gilbert White explains how Timothy formed part of his inheritance in a letter to Daines Barrington from Selborne dated 21 April 1780.

> The old *Sussex* tortoise is become my property. I dug it out of its winter dormitory in *March*, when it was enough awakened to express its resentments by hissing; and, packing it in a box with earth, carried it eighty miles by post-chaises. The rattle and hurry of the journey so perfectly roused it that, when I turned it out on a border, it walked twice down to the bottom of my garden …
>
> This creature sleeps great parts of the summer; for it goes to bed in the longest days at four in the afternoon, and often does not stir in the morning till late. Besides, it retires to rest for every shower; and does not move at all in wet days.
>
> When one reflects on the state of this strange being, it is a matter of wonder to find that Providence should

> bestow such a profusion of days, such a seeming waste of longevity, on a reptile that appears to relish it so little as to squander more than two thirds of its existence in a joyless stupor, and be lost to all sensation for months together in the profoundest of slumbers.

In 1946, the author Sylvia Townsend Warner published extracts from Gilbert White's *Natural History* and *Journals*. From these, we learn that White's tortoise favoured kidney beans and cucumbers and slept under a 'marvel of Peru'. This, according to Karen Bridgman, assistant garden manager for the past seven years at the Gilbert White Museum, is 'a tender perennial with a tuber like a dahlia. It is night scenting and comes out in August.'

It is easy to see at Selborne, as the lawns give way to the fields and woods, divided by a low brick ha-ha, how Timothy tumbled off the ha-ha and made for the hay meadows of the Little and Great Mead beyond. It was here that he was lost for eight days in search of a mate but returned, having met nothing but 'weeds, coarse grass and solitude'.

The diary entries for 1792 give a good idea of the tortoise's life:

> Nov 15th: Timothy comes out.
> Nov 22nd: Timothy comes forth.
> Nov 26th: Timothy hides.
> Dec 4th: Timothy is gone under a tuft of long grass, but is not yet buried in the ground.

Gilbert White died in 1793, and his tortoise a year later. The carapace may now be seen at the Natural History

Museum in London, to which it was presented on 17 April 1853, by Mrs Christopher, Gilbert White's great-niece.

White believed that, in the spring, when the tortoise came out, the swallows would arrive. If the tortoise then buried himself, it would forewarn of a cold spell and the swallows would for its duration go elsewhere.

Like Powderham Timothy, Gilbert White's tortoise was also a girl, but that did nothing to diminish the use of his male name. This discovery was made only after Gilbert White's death.

Two

The Naval Years

'Here goes the last of the Brudenells.'

Lord Cardigan, whose family name is Brudenell-Bruce, Brigade Commander at the Battle of Balaclava in the Crimea, as he led the Charge of the 'Light Brigade'

Gilbert White believed that his tortoise was bought from a sailor in Chichester harbour for half a crown by Mr Snooke. Likewise it is believed that Timothy was a ship's mascot before coming to the safe harbour of the Courtenay family.

'We had always been told that he was at Sebastopol with my forebear,' says 35-year-old Guy Thomas-Everard. John Guy Courtenay-Everard was his great-great-great-uncle, and a portrait of the naval sea captain is in the dining room of his Somerset home. 'My grandmother told my father about his exploits,' continues Thomas-Everard. 'She explained how the tortoise had been with him at Sebastopol and how he had saved some local women from the Cossacks.'

'When he came to us the hole in his shell had already been made from his days as a ship's mascot,' says Lady Gabrielle Courtenay. 'We would never have done that to him.'

Captain John Guy Courtenay-Everard, Timothy's custodian at Sebastopol

She continues, 'You must remember he wouldn't have been very big at this time. He could almost fit in a pocket.' As an omnivore, Timothy was fed on any available scraps and land vegetation. He could also survive for months on end on salt water.

A tortoise as a ship's mascot was highly unusual, but then so was Captain Courtenay-Everard, who was born on 22 September 1831 and brought up at his family seat, Barford Park, in the Quantock Hills in Somerset. He had a countryman's care for adventure and animals.

After Eton, he entered the navy in 1848, passed for mate in 1852 and joined the HMS *Queen* in the Mediterranean. It is here that he adopted Timothy and Timothy adopted him.

They served on the HMS *Queen* at the first bombardment of Sebastopol on 17 October 1854. HMS *Queen* was launched as a three-decker sailing battleship in 1839, with 116 guns and three tall masts.

The first bombardment of the Siege of Sebastopol in which she took part was a disaster for the combined British and French fleet. It was their task to attack the massive forts guarding the seaward approach to Sebastopol as part of the Crimean War. None of the ships could get close enough to the forts to do any extensive damage and they were themselves badly battered by the Russian shells. HMS *Queen* was set on fire three times.

Shortly after his death, *The Times* printed an obituary of

Courtenay-Everard, which gives an insight into his life. At Sebastopol, he met Florence Nightingale, who, with a small band of followers, visited the battery of which he was in command. 'She was as good a woman as any living or dead,' he wrote at the time. She also had her own tortoise, Jimmy, kept as a ward pet at the field hospital at Scutari.

Sadly, or perhaps fortunately, there is no mention of Timothy, but a *Punch* cartoon of the time shows a journalist astride two reined tortoises, galloping ironically at full speed, with the caption: 'The Government Courier with important despatches from the seat of war.' It is possible that this was Jimmy and Timothy.

Jimmy's shell, with a metal shield mounted on its side, can be seen at the Florence Nightingale Museum in London, based at St Thomas's Hospital. He is about 8 inches long by 5 inches wide, with a fine dark carapace.

From *A Centenarian's Memories* we learn that Courtenay-Everard became the oldest living Etonian of his day and surviving officer of the Royal Navy. He was also, at his death, among the few survivors of the Crimea. He left the active list before Lord Jellicoe entered the navy and before Lord Beatty was born.

He served as senior mate on HMS *Queen* before being given his lieutenant's commission 'for saving some women from the Cossacks'. 'My captain told me to take two boats and such men as I wanted and to do our best. It was a tough job getting the women from those rascals. They blazed away at us, and we had to lower the women into our boats by the hair of their heads in some cases. But we brought them safely away.'

Writing at sea off Odessa on 9 September 1854, Captain

W.P. Richards observed the terrain: 'All the birds, and shrubs, with the exception of a few, are like England. The chief things are the tortoises, which are very common here. The French make them into soup and say it is very good, but the English will not touch them.'

Later Courtenay-Everard moved to the HMS *Princess Charlotte*, HMS *Fury* and HMS *Nankin*, seeing active service in the East Indies and China from 1857 to 1860. He received the China Medal and the Taku Clasp. Two years later, he became Inspecting Officer of Coastguard at Whitby, his last naval appointment.

From Courtenay-Everard, Timothy came into the hands of Captain Edward Rutherfoord, a fellow naval officer. The tortoise was already full grown, which puts his age at between forty and fifty at this time, the mid-1880s.

In replying to the naval historian Bert Gedin about Timothy before he came to Powderham, the 17th Earl of Devon's archivist, Lieutenant Colonel Cedric Delforce, wrote in 1999: 'The story is accepted that Captain Rutherfoord was given Timothy by Captain Courtenay-Everard.'

In the Powderham archive is a letter, written on 5 July 1994, by Captain Guy Crowden, RN (Retired), to Cedric Delforce. It is a letter which I unearthed in preparation for the only full interview Timothy was to give. He was 154 at the time, I was 40.

Captain Crowden was of the following opinion: 'It is not inconceivable that Timothy was a long-serving sea-tortoise as well as a companion to Captain Courtenay-Everard.' Crowden points out that Captain Courtenay-Everard was in his hundred and first year when he died on 26 September 1931.

Courtenay-Everard was a worthy custodian of Timothy. In 1887, he succeeded his father to the Barford Park estate near Bridgewater in Somerset. There he was able to enjoy the view of trees planted by his father over ninety years before.

His memories of naval service went back to the era before steam and iron, days in which he used to say the rule was the survival of the fittest.

> Drinking water had to be carried to sea in barrels, and after the ship had been out a fortnight or so 'It stank to Heaven.' One day Everard was seen drinking something that fizzed. An officer approached in alarm and demanded what it was. 'Seidlitz water,' replied Everard, and that, he would add in later years, was the only way in which he could drink ship's water.*
>
> But age and inclemency were no deterrent. In 1880, with his six sons and two daughters, he sailed to New Zealand in *The Lady Joceline*, the last passenger sailing ship that left England for that country.
>
> Until he was nearly ninety, Courtenay-Everard rode to hounds. He had intended to celebrate his hundredth birthday by walking from Barford Park to a meet in a neighbouring village, but, to his great disappointment, he was prevented by slight indisposition.

The meet would have been that of the Devon and Somerset Staghounds, who hunt a greater part of Exmoor to this day. Courtenay-Everards were Masters of the Quarme Harriers, also on Exmoor but now disbanded.

* Seidlitz water was a seltzer drawn from the village mineral spring in Bohemia.

When the *Nankin* docked at Portsmouth, it is supposed that Timothy jumped ship, having heard the next destination was Antarctica. Even the climate of Victorian England was preferable to this frozen fastness. 'I don't know why a naval vessel was going to Antarctica, but it wasn't suitable for a tortoise,' says Lady Gabrielle Courtenay.

The transfer of Timothy from Courtenay-Everard to Edward Rutherfoord happened at this time. And it was to Hampshire, by the green-grey flowing waters of the Itchen, whose famed streams are home to brown trout, that Timothy was brought.

He arrived near the path of the Pilgrim's Way at the Elms, whose terraced gardens were to become his home. But it was not all a Xanadu of tranquillity, as he was to find out.

Three

Land at Last in Hampshire

'While they here sojourn'd, their presence drew us
By the sweetness of their human love.'

Hymn by T.C. Shairp, concluding the Corrie family records

The small Hampshire village of Itchen Abbas is really one long street of detached houses and a population of 250 people. Many of the homes you cannot see behind laurel hedges and neatly fenced fronts, like a green lawn suburb in Connecticut. Each house, however, announces its presence with a sign at the front of the drive, the announcements all painted, carved and engraved into a postman's dream.

The village's residents today are a mixture of the retired and incomers, the latter making their way by car to London early each morning. But once, the B3407, which runs past the church of St John the Baptist, the River Itchen and the towpath of the Pilgrim's Way, was a coaching road from Winchester to Alresford. Earlier, in Chaucerian times, Christian pilgrims would make the 116-mile journey on foot to Canterbury.

At the church, I met a man cutting the grass, Tony Chapman, who led me almost by the cuff of my sleeve to

The cottage at the Elms, Itchen Abbas – home to Timothy and eleven children.

the manor behind. He did not know where the Elms was, but he knew someone who did.

Joan Darntall, who lives at Itchen Abbas Manor, is an investigator's dream and a village's delight. She has lived here for thirty-five years, looks after the church and takes a keen interest in local history. She knew not only the Elms but also Martin Roundell, now ninety, whose wife Louise had been a Corrie and had lived in the house.

As I sat and talked with Martin Roundell in the crepuscular light of his spacious bungalow it was easy to see the herbaceous tranquillity which had been Timothy's home at the Elms below. It was from here, on 18 August 1877, that Thomas Rutherfoord married Harriette Corrie, and that Thomas's very much younger brother Edward, was born in December 1879, who later brought the tortoise into the family in 1892, leaving Timothy there when he went off to sea.

The Elms is a long white residence with walled terraces at the rear and fields and woods beyond that. In front, the prospect looks over the reed beds and waters of the River Itchen. It was built in 1843 for the rector of Itchen Abbas, the Reverend Wright. But when he was succeeded as rector by William Webb Spicer (1850–74), the Bishop of Winchester told him not to use it as it was too small. He moved to the Abbey House near the church. Extensive alterations were made to the Elms in 1851 and the house as it is dates from 1865.

Today it is owned by Stuart and Karen Upcraft and their young family. After toing and froing between back and front door for half an hour I caught up with Karen Upcraft to break the news about her famous former resident. It was bathtime in the early evening for her four children, and she was very good about my unannounced interruption and came outside with her young son to talk to me. He seemed quite uninterested in my news and proceeded to relieve himself on a geranium and my foot as I was talking.

The Upcrafts moved to the Elms from London a year ago. 'We absolutely fell in love with the garden,' said Karen Upcraft. 'I have to admit I don't know a lot about gardening, but I plan to learn. It was Louise Roundell who was such a great gardener, who made it what it is today. I see the garden as being in three distinct zones. There are the front lawns, the paddocks and a small orchard of apple and pear trees with woods at the back, and then, of course, there is the mainly walled garden.' It is not entirely enclosed and we agreed it was a miracle that Timothy did not stray on to the main road below, thirty yards away.

For Timothy, the Elms was a pleasure dome. There

were dressing-up parties, wonderful fruit cages and borders upon which to stroll and dwell, plenty of water and swallows building their nests in the spring. These were the beginnings of Timothy's long days of wine and roses.

All this became clear when Martin Roundell handed me a large red, leather-bound book, entitled 'Records of the Corrie family 1802–1899'. 'Take them and make what you will of them,' he said. I protested at carrying off one of his treasures, but he insisted.

What I discovered was the slow and patient elegance of an age before two world wars, which changed the English landscape and its people for ever. It is easy to see how the arrival of a tortoise would have been regarded, and perhaps therefore go unmentioned, as just another charming diversion in the household.

The gardens at the Elms.

The records were written by Jessie Corrie, another daughter of the house, just as the new century was about to unfold. She was Lady Gabrielle Courtenay's great-aunt. 'I remember meeting her often,' says Lady Gabrielle. 'She was very formidable.' Lady Gabrielle would sit at the window and have tea. On one occasion a squirrel came through the window and upset several cups.

Of the gardens where Timothy lived, Jessie Corrie writes:

> The lawn was so fine, so close, and so springy; tiny little trefoil leaves were there, and 'Crow's Foot', but no plantains. The garden was bounded on the left by a row of stately elms with great rough trunks, up and down which nut-hatches would creep and tap. Below the elms stood some tall firs, veritable ivy-trees, and the home for many birds. Below the firs a beautiful Irish yew, a yew that flourished despite ill-treatment and opposition, for Grannie objected to it. Its head was cut off and only its crimson stump left above ground, and many a kettle of boiling water did Grannie pour upon it after breakfast, making certain it would die. But it lived and flourished and became the home of a tribe of blackbirds and thrushes, and a joy to us grandchildren.
>
> The Irish yew always shewed by its waving plumes which way the wind was blowing, and the yew-blossoms sent out puffs of dusty 'smoke' whenever a bird flew in or out, or the wind was gusty and rough. It made a shelter for a succession of white Persian cats as they madly scampered from the 'Hornbeam' and vanished beneath its boughs, and last, but not least, its shadow was a daily pleasure to watch, for the tree stood like the finger of a dial-plate

> between the lawn and the rising sun.
>
> The light would creep over the Stoke meadows, across the curtain of white mist and the gleaming river, until it reached the east corner of the lawn; then a flood of golden sunlight quickly drank up all the dew, except where the shadow of the Irish yew glittered still with shining drops.
>
> As the sun rose the shadow grew smaller and smaller and at last disappeared, but under the yew the grass seemed always cool and damp, and the clump of spotted dog-tooth violets flourished. I never could decide which pleased me most, the summer shadow dressed with dew, or the winter shadow of white hoar-frost.

But Timothy and the family were in for an abrupt shock. 'My great-grandfather lost all his money,' says Lady Gabrielle Courtenay of John Malcolm Corrie, Harriette's father. 'The family of eleven children had to move into the cottage next door and Timothy went with them.' The Elms was rented out.

What this news meant, however, was that the very spot upon which I was sitting with Martin Roundell, as he sipped a large and well-earned whisky, was Timothy's second real home. 'Timothy was given the run of what had been the vegetable garden for the big house,' he told me.

The cottage was in fact two cottages before Martin Roundell built his own home there in 1987 and the historic edifices were gone for ever. There is a small stone, however, underneath an aubrietia in the wall, which marks the date of their creation at 1865, the same year that the Elms was redesigned.

'I do not know how that enormous number of them

squeezed in,' continues Lady Gabrielle in some disbelief. 'Perhaps some of the elder boys had left home by then.' It may have been out of a sense of duty that they did not, in these straitened circumstances, discard the tortoise.

As can be seen in the churchyard, the Corries were a significant county family who had come to Hampshire from Shropshire. The record ends with the marriage of Harriette Corrie and Thomas Rutherfoord and the death of their beloved grandmother:

> On the 17th we decorated the church, and arranged flowers and fruit at home; melons and grapes, etc., came from Arlington [the big estate near by]. At six o'clock forty-two of the villagers arrived and had dinner on the croquet-ground, and Papa and Tom Rutherfoord made speeches afterwards.
>
> We were a party of thirty-seven ourselves that evening for dinner, and danced afterwards.
>
> On the 18th I was dressed early, and with Nursie ran down to finish the church decorations; then we all had breakfast under the dear old beech-tree on the lawn, and afterwards I dressed Harry's [Harriette's] hair. She looked beautiful, and radiantly happy. Four arches had been erected by the villagers, and the church was crowded, for no lady had been married in Itchen Abbas since Grannie's wedding in 1820.
>
> The bridesmaids waited at the gate for the bride, and Georgie and I held up the white satin train, Dora and Katie walking behind us. Our dresses were of pale blue silk damassé with white muslin fichus and mob caps. The bride and bridegroom drove home after the ceremony, but most of the guests walked, and admired the decorations.

The hand-bell ringers played upon the lawn during breakfast.

Harry's going-away dress was of oatmeal-coloured cloth, braided, with a jacket and cap of the same material. She and her husband went to Ireland for the honeymoon, and then settled in London. We gave a school-treat to all the children in Itchen Abbas to celebrate the wedding-day, and soon afterwards returned to Epsom, where we had a house for a few years.

In 1879 Papa and Mamma, Dora, Katie, and I came back to live at the Elms with Grannie, but we were not together for long. In 1881 dear Grannie became very ill. She faced death with the same steadfast bravery with which she had faced life. No word of complaint ever passed her lips as her strength slipped from her … her last smile was when I laid one of her favourite Malmaison roses on the coverlet by her hand.

In their white smock-frocks the old villagers bore her to her last resting-place under the yew-tree in the churchyard, within the sound of the river.

With Grannie's death a change fell upon the Itchen we knew and loved. She was a living embodiment to us of the past – a link connecting us with those unknown ancestors – a link drawn out of sight, not broken, but without which we feel astray.

Itchen seems still to belong to those who are gone. We seem so intensely modern, but yet responsible to the old owners of the home. There is an unwritten law which makes us each and all keep the house and possessions as nearly as they used to be in olden days, so that married sisters and brothers, if they returned home in the dark, would, I believe, be able to walk after years of absence

> straight to any well-known or loved corner, and lay their hand in certainty upon what used to be found in that place in bygone days.

If only it were true today. Sadly Timothy does not seem to have been in attendance with the white-smocked villagers at the grandmother's funeral. He was, as normal, just in the garden.

But the old aunts, including Jessie Corrie, who never married, had moved back into the Elms. 'My grandmother's sisters just went on living,' recalls Lady Gabrielle Courtenay. 'I went to see the old aunts. Katie died of flu after the First World War, but I met Aunt Jessie and Aunt Dora a lot between the wars at the Elms.'

Cattle with mottled coats still sit among the water meadows and the Itchen soups its molten way through oxbow curves and under small bridges. It is an English landscape of Norman manors and ancient churches.

The nearby M3 motorway makes it difficult to enjoy it in the peace and tranquillity that the Corries and Timothy would have known. But Timothy was once again a step ahead of the march of progress and time. He was about to make another journey to another haven, the Rectory at Honiton in Devon.

FOUR

Timothy Lands with the Courtenays (1900–29)

'He is the creature of my old, deep-seated, and, as it were, impartial conviction.'

Joseph Conrad, *Victory*

When Frederick Leslie Courtenay was born at Powderham on 31 August 1875, he was a third son, and, like so many of his forebears, destined for a life in the church.

By 1935, he was not only the 16th Earl of Devon but also the proud possessor of a castle, an estate and Timothy. For the tortoise had simply arrived one day in a basket at his Devon rectory at Honiton, where he lived with his wife Marguerite and six children, one of whom was an only son, Christopher.

Frederick had married Marguerite Silva of Itchen Abbas in 1907, and this is how Timothy came into his family's hands. Honiton was at this time still famous for its lace, and the appointment was something of a pocket curacy, as the Courtenays still held land and influence here. The present Earl of Devon still has the 'living' here, giving him the right to appoint the vicar. Frederick was also the Mayor of Honiton, a town which still offers a pretty main street and several antiques and tea shops.

Frederick Courtenay had been educated at Exeter College, Oxford, and ordained as a priest by the Bishop of Bath and Wells in 1902. He took up residence as the vicar of Tichborne in Hampshire, not far from Itchen Abbas, in 1904.

Marguerite, wife of the Rev Frederick Courtenay in 1916.

In 1862, this small village had risen to unwanted national prominence through what is known as the case of the Tichborne Claimant. This became a sensational case in the London High Court, lasting 188 days.

The Tichborne heir Roger Charles Doughty-Tichborne had been brought up by his free-thinking mother Henrietta, daughter of Henry Seymour of East Knoyle in Wiltshire, as a Frenchman. His eccentricity and thick French accent led him to banishment and South America. He drowned at sea out of Rio de Janeiro on the *Bella*, which foundered with all hands.

But his mother, Lady Tichborne, remained convinced that her son was still alive and would return to claim his vast inheritance. It was a notion fuelled by her acceptance of a man claiming to be her son. He was, in fact, Tom Castro, a small village butcher from Wagga Wagga in

Queensland, New South Wales.

Only an expensive action in the High Court brought by other members of the Tichborne family ensured that Castro was denounced of his baronetcy and his inheritance. He died in poverty, after ten years of penal servitude, in obscure lodgings in Marylebone, London.

By the time Courtenay took to his pulpit at Tichborne, the case, which dominated the newspapers of Victorian England, had subsided from scandal to history. He was freely at ease to enjoy his parish and the trappings of largesse often afforded to nineteenth-century churchmen when large rectories still abounded and congregations still gathered to hear and fear the parson's learned orisons.

'I think my parents met at a Victorian tennis party,' says Lady Gabrielle Courtenay, who was their fourth daughter. 'My mother and her sisters were all very fond of Timothy, and I heard that they all took turns to look after him, especially Aunt Camilla. She never married, although she was engaged twice. She was a very sweet, pretty lady who became the Victorian support and stay of her family. Both she and her sister Evelyn had been told the story about Timothy being a ship's mascot and not wanting to go to Antarctica.'

In the drawing room of the Briary, the house near Powderham where Lady Gabrielle lives – a wooden gabled house, like a Swiss cottage, which she shared with her late mother and sister Mary – are a table and long wall mirror from the Elms.

'We all knew that Timothy had been brought from Turkey,' says Lady Gabrielle. 'And we knew he had been aboard a ship as a mascot because of the hole which he already had in his shell when he arrived. It was the hole to

The Rev Frederick Courtenay, his wife Marguerite (née Silva), with their six children (back row, left to right) Mary, Evelyn, Gabrielle, (front row, left to right) Angela, Christopher, Kathleen. This picture was taken in 1920, the year that Timothy arrived at Honiton.

tether him. He did not come, as a lot of tortoises did, as some sort of ballast. They used to bring a lot of them over and sell them as pets, but he didn't come like that.'

If Timothy was given first-class treatment in his passage, he certainly repaid the comfort with longevity. He also rewarded his custodians with amusement.

'I must have been about seven when he arrived, because I was still at the age when I played with things in the bath,' says Lady Gabrielle of Timothy's arrival at the Honiton Rectory in 1920. 'My mother was going to Exeter one day and asked me if there was anything I wanted. That day, during my morning bath, someone had the misfortune to step on my celluloid tortoise. So I said I wanted a tortoise, and I was completely misunderstood. Then my grandfather [John Silva] heard that I wanted a tortoise and, since they were moving, Timothy came to Honiton.'

Lady Gabrielle was not a strong child and was sent away to school at St Catherine's in Bude on the north Cornish coast for the sake of her health. When she returned, the tortoise was there.

'The school has now been turned into a car park, which is perhaps just as well as it was a funny place,' recalls Lady Gabrielle. 'I couldn't possibly learn to spell. But then somebody taught me more sensibly, and I got the hang of it in about a fortnight,' she continues.

There was also a governess at home called Miss Platt, but the family called her 'Pipat' for a reason she doesn't recall. 'I had a book called *Reading Without Tears*, which was a list of noises with a picture of an animal at the top and then a whole list of what it was called and where it lived or something. I was left gazing at this. I remember a picture of donkey with the word 'ass' written under it, which wasn't very helpful.'

Frederick and Marguerite Courtenay had come to Honiton shortly after their marriage in 1908. The rectory was a large house with a cook, housemaid, gardener, garden boy and a nanny. 'It was an old-fashioned Victorian household,' says Lady Gabrielle. 'Money was so completely different then. I think the gardener was paid a pound a week. The cook, Mrs Hinton, although she was very fond of me, put us all off eating vegetables for life.'

Lady Gabrielle's parents were Victorians, and she was obliged to attend her father's sermons during matins every

Sunday. 'I believe he preached extremely good sermons. We sat quietly in the pew where we behaved ourselves properly. But I never listened to his sermons – they were quite beyond me. I was just lost in daydreams. I imagined myself being whatever it is that children of that age imagine. I was the hero in all the storybooks, you know. I think everybody does that. My sister Mary was the same.'

But she has fond memories of the rectory. 'We had a wonderful life. Because the rectory was a large house and most of the rooms opened into each other, it was perfect for hide-and-seek. It had a beautiful staircase, a really beautiful staircase and we slid down the banisters. And life just went on day to day, for years really, I suppose.'

Her father did not go to war as he was the vicar and she doesn't remember much about it from her childhood. Lady Katherine Watney still goes back to Honiton to her grandfather's church. 'I look at all the names on the war memorial from that time and think, my father christened most of them. He had to console those familes in their bereavement.'

But Lady Gabrielle does remember Timothy. 'We used to have fun with the tortoise, with Timothy, and he had various things that happened to him.' There was no wall around the Honiton Rectory, but a large lawn which had two tennis courts, a ha-ha at the bottom, a sort of fence and farmland beyond.

'Timothy had to be restricted, because he used to disappear, and we used to have to have "Timothy hunts" every so often,' she recalls. 'And a piece of string was tied through his hole and he had another end of it tied to a child's wooden hoop, such as we all had in those days. That slowed him down, but he used to get terribly tangled around things like rose bushes and we used to have to untangle him. And he dug himself little banks all around the lawn and he dug himself a hole. He changed his hole every few months.

'The garden was a square, and there were sort of banks on three sides of it really, with the ha-ha at the bottom. It was a sort of double bank, so that you could sit on the lower one, and he had to get into the lower one but wasn't able to climb the bank, so we used to have to rescue him. And, of course, in the wintertime he wasn't there. He buried himself and there was none of this putting him away in a box.

'I remember he got something the matter with his hind legs. The hole in his shell was invaded by ants. I remember my mother going out and bathing his hind legs. He always knew her voice and would come to her. I think it was with boracic powder mixed with water. Then she would soothe him with Pond's Extract, which she usually put on us. Pond's was wonderful if you twisted your ankle or anything. It's lovely and cooling because it's a sort of liquid. It's a lovely smell and the smell did Timothy and us a lot of good.'

At Honiton, Timothy was very much left to fend for himself. 'Oh, we fed him,' says Lady Gabrielle, 'but he walked around the lawn and the garden was pretty wild, so there was quite a bit of clover in the lawn. I think he did eat buttercups, but he did like dandelions and we had lovely dandelions.

'I used to like to feed him stalk first and when he reached the flowerhead he used to get a lovely yellow moustache and this entertained us. And then he got wise to that actually, so we had to take to putting two dandelions head to tail, so he ate the flowerhead and then he had to go munching up the two stalks to reach the other. To get him started we had to give him one flowerhead because, I have to say, he wasn't always hungry.'

Timothy didn't hiss like Gilbert White's tortoise, but he had another slightly unfortunate habit. 'He was rather unpleasant when he overate on strawberries,' says Lady Gabrielle. 'Only "unpleasant" because it upset his insides. If we were having tea in the garden and he was rather near after he had eaten too many strawberries, he had to be removed.'

Life at the Honiton Rectory during the 1920s was a reflection of what was happening all over England as a result of the Great War. It was a time of austerity and change, from which many families and houses never recovered.

But Lady Gabrielle recalls, 'We didn't ride the pony but took it out with the cart to the surrounding villages where the wild daffodils grew and picked them to decorate the church for Easter. I suppose it was my mother doing it really, and that we were only getting under foot. It was a lovely life really. There were no awful cars rushing along the roads. In fact there wasn't even tarmac.'

Lady Gabrielle remembers tarmac being laid in Honiton and the long-since-departed cattle market. 'We used to have to shut the rectory gate; otherwise the cows and sheep being driven to market would have got into the garden. I once took some pigs to market, when I was bigger, but they got loose in the council house gardens.' The Courtenays did not farm as such, but Gabrielle's mother had taken in some animals and an in-calf Guernsey cow before the war, which was milked by the gardener.

It was after the Great War that Lady Gabrielle saw the greatest changes of her life. 'We were still there but we had fewer and fewer people to wait upon us, in fact none at all. We had less and less money, and my father's stipend didn't go up, so we did all the cooking and everything by the time we left Honiton. It was an enormous transition, brought on by the Great War.'

There were still entertainments to enjoy. 'Because nobody had a car, you had to make your own fun much more, which in a way was more fun,' says Lady Gabrielle. 'We used to get involved with the Honiton carnival once a year, and the Honiton fair used to come, with roundabouts – that was a great thing in our lives.'

All the family looked forward to the Christmas pantomime in Exeter. Lady Gabrielle remembers watching her first performance of *Ali Baba and the Forty Thieves*. 'I must have been very small because I was very indignant that there weren't enough thieves, there weren't forty of them. And I asked my mother where the men were, because they were all little girls, and she said: "The men are busy working the machinery."'

If there were innocent treats for the children, so were there for Timothy. The Rev Frederick and Marguerite Courtenay and the family would holiday regularly at Powderham and at a seaside boarding house at Dawlish during the 1920s. Timothy was taken with them, in a wicker basket, to beaches that in those days were still owned by the family.

'We didn't have a car, so he had to travel with us by train,' says Lady Gabrielle. 'We used to catch a train at Honiton, and had to buy all sorts of tickets. It was quite a performance, and my mother used to go and buy the tickets, and we had various other things, besides the tortoise. We had dogs, so we had to buy a dog ticket. This was for my father's shooting spaniel, Sooty. We even had to get a ticket for the pram.' Was there a special ticket for Timothy? 'Yes, yes, there was. It was something of a family joke because my mother used to say with a face as solemn as could be to the collector: "And do I *have* to have a reptile ticket?"'

The family would take the steam train to Exeter, then change to go on to Starcross. It must have been of assistance that the family had permission to hold up the train at their own station for as long as they liked. From Powderham, they would take lodgings at Dawlish, not far from the sandy beaches and warm waters of the south coast. Timothy was not required to bathe – tortoises are notoriously bad at swimming – nor to sunbathe. 'We just left him in the garden at the boarding house,' recalls Lady Gabrielle.

Timothy took up fulltime residence at Powderham when the Rev Frederick Courtenay became the 16th Earl in 1935. Whether because he was left too long to his own devices on these holidays or because he had a desire to relive the excitement of his youth – Timothy was by now in his eighties – there occurred at this time something of a dark incident in his life. 'This is when,' says Lady Gabrielle, with the long pause of someone about to impart the secret of a dusty family skeleton, 'this is when Timothy got *drunk*.

'It was in the garden at Powderham. In those days there were a lot of azaleas, yellow azaleas, I think they were. And they smell absolutely intoxicating, and Timothy ate them, ate the blossom as it fell. My mother found Timothy on the lawn, with his head lying out on the cool grass, absolutely drunk. She dosed him with castor oil. It must have been after breakfast because she went out, I suppose, after all the workers.

'My uncle Charlie, my father's oldest brother, was living at Powderham then, and they had a married couple, Clapton and Mrs Clapton, as butler and cook. She was a marvellous woman, really marvellous. She must have been much younger than him because she went on for years and years. I remember her until just before the Second World War.

The 14th Earl, Uncle Charlie, with his nephew Christopher, the spaniels and Timothy at Powderham on holiday in the 1920s.

'Clapton appeared at my mother's side, saying he couldn't find one of the teaspoons and had she seen it. And she said, "Oh yes, I've got it here, I've got it here, I'm just dosing the tortoise with it." He was probably shocked. My dear mother, she was not quite as conventional as she was supposed to be.

'I know I am bound to say this as her daughter, but everybody loved her, even though she had her Victorian upbringing. She wasn't a conventional woman. What she would think today of what goes on, I cannot imagine … the way the young are … I don't mean all the young, but these binge-drinking parties and that sort of thing. Well, I think she would be horrified. As for the language people use quite openly nowadays, I should think she would be turning in her grave like anything.'

Nor indeed was Timothy as conventional as he was supposed to be. In 1926, he was taken by 'Uncle Charlie', then the 14th Earl of Devon, to the Zoological Society of London, of which he was a fellow. What railway passengers made of a peer carrying a tortoise can only be guessed at.

What passed at the Zoological Society was astounding. The purpose of the visit was to see if Timothy could mate. In order to do this, the curators of the Department of Herpetology had to take the preliminary step of establishing Timothy's sex. From beneath their learned stares, the tortoise must have looked up with some bewilderment. For Timothy was, in fact, like Gilbert White's tortoise before him, really a Timothea.

For all White's watching of his tortoise, it was only when he was examined after his death that he was found out to be female, so White was spared this information. Like White's tortoise, Timothy's name was never changed.

'Years later, attempts were made to mate Timothy with another tortoise called Toby,' recalls Lady Gabrielle. 'It was not successful, although he did form something of an attachment to my brother Christopher's wartime helmet.' To this day, the helmet that saved Christopher Devon's life in North Africa (there is the hole where a bullet went through the top) is known affectionately as 'Timothy's boyfriend'.

Lady Gabrielle Courtenay being presented at Court in 1931.

In 1931, Frederick Courtenay deemed it important that his daughter Gabrielle, now aged eighteen, should go to London to be presented at Court. It was still then the custom for debutantes to go to Buckingham Palace and curtsey before George V and Queen Mary.

'We all dressed up in white with things in our hair,' she remembers. 'It was hot and we had to wait in our cars for hours in the courtyard, so our bouquets wilted.'

Lady Gabrielle stayed with a cousin and was not really sure why she was there. 'We were terribly poor, but I just went.' Eventually, the debutantes were let in by the front door of the palace, and sat with their parents in rows.

'It was like a confirmation, I suppose,' continues Lady Gabrielle, 'although it wasn't quite like church. It was very exciting and all seemed so grand to a country girl. George

V was very unwell – I could see that. I went into the Throne Room and curtsied. The King and Queen didn't say a word.' Afterwards there was a buffet lunch. 'I remember the enormous salt cellars on the table. Then we just went home.'

But there was something worth coming home for. At this time Lady Gabrielle would holiday with her sister Angela in Cornwall. They took up surfing, little realising that their efforts on wooden boards would one day become a worldwide sport. 'We stayed with Mrs Gurney at Port Gaverne,' recalls Lady Gabrielle. 'She would give us a Thermos and picnic every day.' She admits to not having been very good at surfing by today's standards. 'I knew when to catch a wave at the right moment, and how to come in on it lying down.'

Once she was told off by the local policeman for driving a car on the beach – shades of Cornish surfing life all too familiar today. Timothy, not being keen on water, did not accompany her.

Later the Honiton Rectory was demolished and turned into a housing estate. All that remains, and this can be seen from the road into the High Street approached from Exeter, is a tree. It is a giant cedar on which Lady Gabrielle Courtenay played as a child.

FIVE

Powderham before the Second World War

'Probably no title in the peerage has undergone such a variety of changes. It has become extinct five times, once it lapsed for 300 years, and its owners have suffered all sorts of vicissitudes.'

Daily Courier, 7 February 1927

When Timothy came back from the Zoological Society of London, there ended perhaps the last great age of innocence for the family and for the estate. Over the next decade or so, three Earls of Devon would die and their heir, Christopher, would marry his cousin's wife in circumstances that forced him to resign his commission from the Coldstream Guards. It was a decade in which Gibbon's observation of the family motto, 'Where have I fallen, what have I done?', as one of plaintiveness which deplores the fall of the ancient house, was never more true.

On 8 February 1927, Charles Pepys Courtenay, the 14th Earl, died. He had remained a bachelor, having been disappointed in love. He held a ball at Powderham in order to propose, but the girl on whom he had set his heart chose that night to tell him she was marrying someone else.

Then, in 1935, the middle brother Henry, who had succeeded him, and who had been rector of Powderham (1904–27), died unmarried. Not five months later, Frederick, briefly the 16th Earl, also died, at the age of fifty-nine. He was taken ill at Windsor, where he was to give a talk at Eton. In the first month of his earldom, he had organised a family gathering to celebrate the 600th anniversary of the granting of the title, but this had to be abandoned on the grounds of his declining health.

The deaths in quick succession were a calamity for the estate and the family, with three sets of death duties being levied in just over eight years. The rate of inheritance tax was penal and, as Lady Katherine Watney says, 'None of the family thought of ways of avoiding death duties.'

So an estate and landholding – including historic houses, villages, farms, lodges and cottages which in 1905 had stood at 55,000 acres, making it perhaps the largest in Devon – was, by 1955, reduced to 5,000 acres. Today the Powderham estate is 3,500 acres and only now have the earlier death duties finally been paid off.

The figures for death duties levied on the two deaths in 1935 show the dramatic reduction in the estate. When the 15th Earl died, the estate was valued at £308,979, for which £92,700 was paid in tax. For Frederick Devon, the 16th Earl, the estate was valued at only £62,479, and the duty was approximately £10,000.

One of the first unavoidable tasks for Christopher Devon on assuming the earldom in 1935 at the age of twenty was to sell Ford House in Newton Abbot. It had been in the family for generations, and both Charles I and William of Orange had stayed there.

As if Christopher Devon did not have enough to

contend with, he was then subjected in 1936 to his own version of the Tichborne Claimant. A clerk-in-charge of the wardrobe at film studios in Denham, Buckinghamshire, came forward to claim the earldom. 'I claim to be the Earl of Devon by direct descent,' wrote the clerk, Austin Denis Harry Courtenay, to Christopher Devon. 'I have never known this claim to be disputed, although I am aware of the fact that Powderham Castle and other estates are in the hands of another branch of the family.'

Austin Courtenay was quickly investigated by the newspapers, who interviewed him in the costume department where he worked. Before the reporter for the *Sunday Express*, Gwyn Lewis, was allowed to put his questions, however, Courtenay said, looking up from the desk where he was writing: 'Just let me fill in this requisition for a dozen pairs of silk stockings for Marlene Dietrich.'

Courtenay was forty-three, a father of seven, who had fought in the war and had various jobs as butcher's boy, postman, labourer, milk roundsman and gardener. His peripatetic career sounds familiar among those living in the changed and insecure post-war world of the 1920s.

Perhaps for this reason, the real Earl of Devon was sympathetic. When approached by the intrepid Gwyn Lewis, he answered him thoughtfully: 'I am certain my right to the title is unassailable but, if you will give me particulars of the claimant's family, I will go carefully through our genealogical papers this weekend, and see if there is the slightest doubt to my right.'

No court case ensued, and nothing became of the claim. Austin Courtenay always believed he was the rightful claimant and that, had his father not lost a few important papers, he should be in residence at Powderham. It is possible he just really wanted to get his hands on the tortoise, an aspect of his inheritance he cleverly neglected to mention. But if Christopher Devon was good to the newspapers, they were not good to him in what followed. And a court case very much ensued.

In 1939, Christopher Devon married, at the age of only twenty-three. His bride, Venetia, was nine years his senior, and had already been married, to his cousin the 6th Earl of Cottenham, a regarded motor-racing correspondent. She is said to have attracted the attentions of the Duke of Windsor, with her height, beauty and black hair.

Lord Cottenham had raced Alvises with Sir Henry Segrave at Brooklands before the latter was killed powerboat racing on Windermere in Cumberland in 1930. He had also advised the Police College at Hendon on advanced driving techniques.

The Cottenhams had two daughters, Lady Rose, born in 1927, and Lady Paulina, born three years later. The Cottenham family name is Pepys (pronounced 'Pep-is'). The diarist Samuel Pepys was a forebear, but he idiosyncratically insisted upon pronouncing his name 'Peeps'.

The 6th Earl of Cottenham and 17th Earl of Devon shared a great-grandfather, the 1st Earl of Cottenham, the Lord Chancellor. Such was the closeness of the family that Lady Rose remembers the Reverend Frederick Courtenay and his wife Marguerite coming to stay with her parents in London at their Hampstead home. 'He would come and sit on the end of the bed and let us play with his mayoral chain. Although we only met him once as children, we both cried when he died,' recalls Lady Rose.

'When Christopher and Venetia first met, she was a

bride and he was a prep-school boy with a puppy stuffed down his shirt,' continues Lady Rose. 'When he went to London, my parents looked after him. My mother never guessed that this nineteen-year-old would fall in love with her and that she would fall in love with him.'

Christopher and Venetia Devon were married in July 1939, but not before several newspapers had reported the details of the divorce. 'A Brighton hotel bill and a confession that she was in love with the co-respondent were mentioned when the Earl of Cottenham was awarded a decree nisi in London yesterday on the grounds of his wife's misconduct with the Earl of Devon, his cousin,' reported the *Daily Mail* on 14 January 1939.

Whatever the circumstances of the marriage, Lord Devon felt obliged to resign his commission from the Coldstream Guards. It was then a regimental rule that should any officer be cited as a co-respondent in a divorce case, he must leave their company immediately.

Rose and Paulina Pepys were eleven and nine when their mother brought them to Powderham, but they had visited several times before as cousins. 'Powderham never felt like a strange place, and we loved the peace and beauty,' says Lady Rose. 'We weren't too young to appreciate that.'

Their father, meanwhile, had moved to America, as a secret agent for MI5 in charge of transport. He wanted to have the children in America, but another court case settled them with their mother. The liner in which they were to have sailed was torpedoed. Lord Cottenham later died at the age of forty from a weak heart, brought on by rheumatic fever suffered as a child.

'My father cared so much, he wanted us to be perfect,' says Lady Rose. 'We wrote to him each week and he would

(left to right) Lady Paulina and Lady Rose Pepys with Pipit the cairn terrier in 1939.

return the letters, marked in red ink, admonishing us for our spelling and grammar. So, unjustly, and I will admit it, we preferred our stepfather. We loved him more than our own father. He was the loveliest stepfather you could imagine.

'Our stepfather never set us an example, which was an example in itself. He was like a little boy. He taught us kindness and tolerance to animals. From my mother I got a heightened sense of social conscience, which made me want to become a nurse.'

The children were educated by a small, fiery free-French governess called Mademoiselle Cothard, whom the family called 'Mallo', and who also taught Lady Devon to cook. Besides teaching the two girls to knit for the war effort, she dug her own vegetable patch and lived to be ninety-two – another example of the longevity of Powderham residents and those associated with Timothy.

Mallo, the French governess at Powderham, who looked after Timothy. (Reproduced courtesy of the Solent News and Photo Library.)

Mademoiselle Cothard did not return to France after the war, and is buried in the Powderham Church of St Clement, patron saint of sailors. As befits an estuary church, the fouled anchor of his emblem may be seen there.

The day war was declared, Rose fell off her bicycle and rushed into the castle, crying that her nose was broken. Her mother, grandparents and French governess were listening to the Prime Minister's broadcast, her nine-year-old sister on her mother's lap. 'I was passed a handkerchief and told to keep quiet,' she remembers. 'I too then listened to the tired, flat voice of Neville Chamberlain telling the nation that a state of war now existed between Germany and England.' It was Sunday 3 September 1939.

Earlier, they had all been to church and prayed for peace. 'Our stepfather had left for London after breakfast,' says Lady Rose. 'I clearly recall his look of despair as he drove off.'

Lord Devon returned to the Coldstream Guards. 'I was not invited to come back, I merely did so,' he said at the time. He had got round the rules, and so had his regiment, by allowing him to rejoin through the Reserve List. Manpower had become more important than the Guards' code.

While he was stationed for training near Sandringham in Norfolk, an invitation was issued for officers to shoot with George VI. Lord Devon and one or two other officers in similar personal circumstances, were not invited. Word went round that these officers 'were good enough to shoot his Majesty's enemies, but not his pheasants'. When the King got to hear of it he extended his invitation to them as well.

Christopher Devon rejoined the Coldstream Guards as a second lieutenant and fought in Belgium and France, and was evacuated from Dunkirk in June 1940. He escaped through the German-held town of Roubaix dressed as a French cowherd, driving his cattle before him.

In 1942, he went to North Africa as a captain, was wounded on Christmas Day, and mentioned in dispatches. Immediately the war ended, he once again resigned his commission and returned to Powderham.

If his marriage to Venetia Devon had begun among a shower of rain – and it should be remembered that tortoises do not like rain – then the enduring love that they had for each other more than rewarded the courage of their decision.

Six

The Second World War

'None of us liked the bombs.'

Captain R.N.C Knight Bruce, Sunday 21 June, 1997

My father said these words over Sunday lunch on a summer's day, while talking about a fellow officer who had been sent back from the battlefields of North Africa in 1942. The officer's excuse was that he didn't like the bombs. Two days later my father died.

I think my father's friendship with the 17th Earl of Devon stemmed not just from the fact that they had nearby estates but also from the fact that as young men they had both been to war in North Africa. But while Lord Devon left Powderham for the war – his wartime helmet, 'Timothy's boyfriend', now sits on a table in the ante-room at Powderham and tells the story of his courage and survival – the war did not leave Powderham.

In what seemed like nightly raids, bombs were dropped on nearby Exeter, once the jewel of the south-west with its gracious Georgian terraces like those of Bath and Edinburgh. Powderham was plunged into darkness with blackout sheets covering all the windows.

Nothing could save the silhouette of the roof against the

(left to right) At Powderham in the courtyard in 1940: Lady Devon, Mrs P. Gunter, Mrs J.V. Taylor, Sorel Gunter, Captain J.V. Taylor, Paulina Pepys, Chinkie Gunter, Rose Pepys and Eddie Pitt. (Reproduced courtesy of the Solent News and Photo Library.)

water in a full or 'hunter's' moon, giving away its presence to the German bombers. Yet for some reason, the castle was spared.

It snowed during the Christmas of 1940 and the children snowballed in the courtyard and nursed their sick cairn terrier. In the spring came, with glorious sunshine, and in the autumn Christopher and Venetia Devon's eldest child Katherine was born.

Lady Paulina can remember the nurserymaids running down from the roof, where they were airing clothes and linen. 'They had seen a plane with swastikas on it investigating the castle,' she recalls. 'It later strafed and killed a farmhand in Kenton.'

From their bedroom in the north tower of the castle,

they could look down on to the Rose Garden below, where Timothy lived. 'We used to love to watch his nightly peregrinations,' says Lady Rose.

It was during these look-outs that they noticed a phenomenon. Of his own accord and, as always, left to the elements, Timothy decided to take matters into his own hands. 'He built an air-raid shelter where he had never dug before,' explains Lady Gabrielle Courtenay. 'I think he was disturbed by the reverberations of the bombs dropping. He dug it under the stone steps in the garden. It was not very deep, but he was protected by the bottom step.'

After the war and the restoration of peace, Timothy simply returned to his lodgings under the purple wisteria and hibernated in the normal way.

Powderham was never requisitioned during the war and it miraculously escaped a direct hit by bombing. But, as in so many areas of life, the castle felt the effects of war which were to change its daily life for ever. The roof suffered extensive pitting from the fall-out of anti-aircraft barrages, as a result of which it eventually had to be replaced. One of the conditions of a Ministry of Works grant was that the house should be opened to the public.

Was there a special reason why Powderham was spared when Exeter was bombed almost nightly?

In 1881, Edward Wood, the fourth son of the 2nd Viscount Halifax, was born at Powderham. His mother was Lady Agnes Courtenay, only daughter of the 11th Earl of Devon, and she always returned from her home in Yorkshire to the castle to have her children.

Wood went on to become Viceroy of India (1926–31) and Foreign Secretary (1938–41) and, in 1944, was created the 1st Earl of Halifax. One day, he inadvertently told

George VI that he had been born in Devon as the two travelled there by train. As the historian Andrew Roberts records in *The Holy Fox: the Life of Lord Halifax*, 'He soon regretted it, when the king, displaying all his heavy Hanoverian drollness, pointed to every shack and cow-shed along the way, asking, "Is that where you were born, Edward?" until the butt of his constantly reiterated joke found it hard to continue his courtly laughter.'

As Foreign Secretary, Halifax initially supported Prime Minister Neville Chamberlain's stance of appeasement with Hitler. In 1937, Halifax met Hitler, ostensibly because they were both attending an International Hunting Exhibition in Berlin. Halifax was Master of the Middleton foxhounds in Yorkshire (although Hitler was a vulpicide).* The German for 'View halloo' is '*Halali*', so Halifax was nicknamed 'Halalifax' by the German newspapers, a pun the Berliners found very funny. Halifax mistook Hitler for a footman and was about to hand him his hat and coat before a German aide hissed into his ear: '*Der Führer! Der Führer!*' Hitler, for his part, dismissed Halifax as 'the English parson'.

Whether or not Halifax discussed Powderham – or indeed Timothy – with Hitler, the Führer let it be known that upon his successful conquest of Britain he would use Powderham as his West Country base. 'We were told this by our cousin Alan Lennox-Boyd after the war,' recalls Lady Rose.

'Germany had strict instructions to spare Powderham,' she continues. On Halifax's visit to Germany, he had met Hermann Goering, Commander-in-Chief of the German

* A vulpicide is someone who kills foxes but not by means of hounds – i.e. he shoots them. The term comes from J.K. Stanford's novel *Death of a Vulpicide*.

air force, and they got on well, as Halifax recorded in his diary. 'Goering's personality was frankly attractive, like a great schoolboy ... a composite personality – film star, great landowner interested in his estate, Prime Minister, party manager, head gamekeeper at Chatsworth.'

Lady Gabrielle Courtenay remembers meeting Lord Halifax at Powderham after the war. 'I am going to speak to you in French,' he said to her one night at dinner. '"I have to be warned if I am going to speak French," I replied, quite firmly, and refused to do so. You see, we only ever did written French with our governess.'

As it turned out, Powderham was used weekly for knitting parties where the children got to know the wives of the estate workers. They were making socks at ten years old.

'As I grew bigger, and Mummy became even more immersed in running Powderham, and in her duties as Vice-President of the South Devon Red Cross, I was delegated the task of village visiting,' says Lady Rose. 'I loved this.'

The State Dining Room had more glamorous uses. Officers from a Scottish regiment were billeted at the castle for a time. Briefly, too, it was headquarters for an American force. Rose was allowed to drive a jeep at fifteen without supervision.

General Sir Oliver Leese also spent some nights before departing for North Africa in 1943 as the general commanding the 30 Corps in North Africa. 'The courtyard was full of tanks and armoured cars,' recalls Lady Rose. Sir Oliver Leese was later to succeed General Montgomery as Commander-in-Chief of the 8th Army in Italy.

The State Dining Room was the ideal officer's mess during these various visitations. 'Mummy often entertained officers from a Polish air force squadron [the Eagle Owls] based at Exeter,' says Lady Rose. 'Some of them spent their leave with us.'

The Luftwaffe became an increasing part of life in rural Devon. 'In 1942 we had our first taste of real fear,' says Lady Rose. 'The German bombers throbbed their way overhead. We heard them come over, and often we heard them return, when they would unload leftover bombs anywhere they saw fit.' The children were taken down to sleep in the cellars.

At the height of the Exeter Blitz on 5 May 1942, Hugh Rupert Courtenay, Christopher Devon's only son and heir, was born in the state bed at Powderham. Lord Halifax was appointed his godfather. No beacons were lit, because it was wartime. 'He bellowed like the fat bulls of Basan,' says Lady Rose who was in the nearby north tower. Her sister turned to her and said: 'It's got to be a boy. No girl would make that row.'

The baby should have been born in Exeter but that was not possible because of the bombing. Mallo kept vigil, under great stress. The telephones went dead, and there was no means of contacting the family doctor, Dr Mackie. 'Suddenly, the front door bell rang,' remembers Lady Rose. 'Mallo answered it, rather scared. There stood Dr Mackie, with his wife and small children. The bombs had proved too much for their youngest child, and he knew Mummy must need him soon.'

Lady Devon was heard to remark after the birth: 'Poor little heir. No church bells. No fireworks.' The baby weighed ten pounds and was christened in the castle chapel.

The children in wartime became adept at amusing themselves. Paulina knew every inch of the park and, at twelve, mapped it, having ridden its length and breadth on her Dartmoor pony. Rose rode an old charger given to her by an uncle.

In the winter when friends visited they played hide-and-seek all over the castle. 'All those friends are still alive, and recall the fun we had,' says Lady Rose. She invented 'the Black Beetle Secret Society' for the children, which flourished in the cellars. She also invented stories for Katherine and Hugh, inspired by the park with its dewpond, heronry, fallow and Japanese deer and herd of South Devon cattle.

They also chased rats around the cellars with rolled-up newspapers. 'Mummy always refused to come to the cellars,' recalls Lady Rose.

Lady Devon and her children Katherine and Hugh play with Timothy in the Powderham Rose Garden in 1943.

Then there were holidays and outings with the children spending a month on Dartmoor and Exmoor. There were picnics watched by the wild ponies that roam there, trips to Bude and Polzeath, and learning about the legends of King Arthur at Tintagel.

During the war, Lady Gabrielle Courtenay enlisted as a nurse for the Red Cross. She was then living in a house that her mother had rented near Powderham, in Ottery St Mary. 'It wasn't always such fun. Horrifying sometimes. It is surprising what the Red Cross did during the war. Why they don't make use of them now, I can't imagine,' she says.

'I didn't go abroad because by that time my mother wasn't strong. I spent part of my time at the top of Woodbury Common at Bystock House, which was a convalescent home, where I cooked for the troops. And then my inside got upset – I suppose it was my own cooking. I wouldn't be surprised, with what we had to cook in those days.'

Gabrielle was transferred for six months to a children's hospital outside Bristol. 'I was there for the Battle of Britain. I was on night duty and the sky was black with our planes going over for the invasion. I have never forgotten that night, the constant circling and the noises of the planes.'

She was working at Bystock when Hugh was born and Exeter was being bombed. The printing works for Exeter's *Express & Echo* had been moved to Powderham to the indoor riding school so that it could still be printed. 'I remember walking over the rubble of the cathedral. That's when it all struck home to us,' says Lady Gabrielle. 'A painting of Jesus which we were all fond of had been destroyed.'

Bedford Circus, the once majestic Georgian sweep which gave Exeter so much of its architectural pride and importance, was flattened. Those buildings which remained defiant, tattered remnants of a gentler age, fell under the swinging ball of demolition. 'I didn't much like Bedford Circus,' Lady Gabrielle admits. 'You see, that's where I had to go to the dentist as a child.'

She was fonder of Deller's tea rooms in Bedford Street, which was destroyed by an oil bomb. This was a grand tea shop, to which she would be taken by her mother. 'It was an enormous place where we went and had cakes. It was all tiers and tables, with two lots of galleries all the way round. You went up this rather grand twisting staircase of stone and you could look down on the people below. But the tragedy was that Exeter was flat, absolutely flat.'

Lady Gabrielle Courtenay celebrated VJ Day at the end of the war in London in August 1945 in her nurse's uniform. She also attended the state opening of Parliament as the sister and daughter of a peer.

'I was travelling on the Underground to meet my mother at her club, the Forum, when I heard the cheers above,' she recalls. 'I was very unknowing about London and when I had to ask a man how to change trains I asked him if this meant the war was over, which it did.'

At the state opening of Parliament, she visited the House of Commons, sitting in the Strangers' Gallery. 'I sat down with the wives of new MPs,' she recalls. 'The woman sitting next to me asked if I was one of them and I replied no, my father used to be in the House of Lords. She looked rather surprised. It was a wonderful weekend because London went crazy. My brother had a car, and of course they were a lot more dressed up than I was, and we drove away and the crowd cheered at us like mad, as if we were famous.'

Paulina and Rose were also taken to London by their mother 'to go mad with the crowds'. 'Several people fainted in the throng around Buckingham Palace and she gave them first aid,' says Lady Rose of her mother, who was wearing her Red Cross uniform. 'Our stepfather joined us in khaki, not yet demobbed. The royal family, on the balcony with Winston Churchill, received roars of acclaim. Princess Elizabeth was slim and lovely in ATS uniform.'

The family returned to Powderham, to the usual church fête in the garden. It was a glorious afternoon in a country at peace. In the Marble Hall were barrels of 'scrumpy', as Devon cider is known. Rose had several glasses, and her younger sister warned her not to get drunk. 'If you drink any more of that you'll be wonky,' Paulina said to Rose. 'She was right, but, at seventeen, I knew best. Glaring, I poured myself some more, and regretted it. On the terrace was an American officer whom I thought "a dish". We made a date for that evening, when a dance was held in the castle. He brought a friend, to partner Paulina, and they had a lovely time. We did not, for the cider finally overcame me. As I danced around, I slept on his shoulder. Thus did I ruin my first dance and date of peacetime.'

Christopher Devon also returned to Powderham. 'I think he came back and set about becoming an old man,' says Lady Rose. 'He didn't forget his experiences in North Africa and he brooded on them.' It must have been some solace to see something as simple as a tortoise in the garden.

My father also came back from North Africa, having spent a year in an Italian prisoner-of-war camp. He walked

600 miles through German-occupied Italy to return home for Christmas in 1943. Like Christopher Devon, he never talked about it or his feelings on seeing Exeter destroyed by bombs. But bombs, when they have fallen, have a habit of still going off, even in silence.

SEVEN

The Post-war Years: 1945–60

> ‘“Victory” was the last word I had written in peace-time. It was the last literary thought which had occurred to me before the doors of the Temple of Janus flying open with a crash shook the minds, the hearts, and consciences of men all over the world.’
>
> Joseph Conrad, *Victory*

If Lord Devon was a changed man after the war, one of his traits remained constant throughout his life. This was his absolute refusal to open, let alone answer, letters.

‘I think one of his school reports from Winchester said he was “idle”,’ says his daughter, Lady Katherine Watney. ‘Anyway, it was not uncommon to find letters addressed to him stuffed in all corners of his car, which was itself like a dog kennel.’ Many will recognise these as familiar character traits among aristocratic English country-men.

But on one matter Lord Devon was most enthusiastic. This was when he was obliged to catch raindrops from the castle’s leaking roof or, better still, clamber on to the roof itself to empty the gutters. ‘He got on his overalls and had a special bucket and bowler hat known as “His Lordship’s plumber’s hat,”’ says Lady Katherine. It wasn’t the one he

A family picnic in 1947: Lord Devon, Lady Paulina Pepys, Lady Devon, Katherine and Hugh Courtenay.

used for Haldon Races, but green with age, the patina of a tortoiseshell. 'He found it much easier when it was raining than using an umbrella.'

But behind this humour lay the stark reality of a world changed for ever. Rationing, bereavement, the destruction of Exeter and little money or men on the land had replaced the familiar landscape in post-war Devon.

Around the country many estates went under, simply submerged in an unequal fight of heredity against progress. Lawyers from London wrote unsolicited letters to landowners offering cash for land at terms advantageous to them and their moneyed city clients. Often, the local solicitor was encouraged to act against the landowner's interests, recommending that they sell.

Tenants who had not fought in the war bought land

from ageing squires whose sons had died. 'What Hitler did not destroy, the lawyers did' was the saying of our grandparents after the war, and plenty in the present generation of landowners remember this today.

It gave rise to a culture of doing nothing, not through lack of enterprise, but because of a fear of the new, a fear of further losses. It also gave rise to a loss of contentment and continuity.

Devon, with its smaller estates, was as badly affected as any county. If those families today appear even keener to hold on to them, to support each other at county shows or public gatherings, their reasons are understandable. They have a shared tragedy in their inheritance.

Powderham was too large to be a home, yet it could not sustain itself and its expensive running costs on depressed agricultural tenancies. 'After the war it was the same for everybody,' says Lady Katherine. 'You just had the odd old boy working at the castle and the gamekeeper.'

For the Courtenays there wasn't the option of standing still and doing nothing, or else the estate, which had already been reduced by nine-tenths since the turn of the twentieth century, would indeed become little better than a billet for the Führer.

It was Lady Devon who is credited with the vision, energy and determination to try anything to keep the estate, and in particular the castle, going. She and Lord Devon decided to open a country house hotel, taking a ninety-nine-year lease on a large house in nearby Kenton. This was to be a gentleman's hotel, the sort which after the war people could stay in to forget their own losses of family and property.

'They were amateurs in a professional world and it did

not work,' says Lady Katherine. 'You had to pay the staff different rates for lunch and dinner, and I don't think they fully understood this.' Perhaps Lord Devon, with his disinterest in matters written, also had difficulty with the order book.

'She was very good and very determined,' says Lady Gabrielle Courtenay of her sister-in-law. In 1947, Gabrielle moved to the Briary with her elder sister Mary and their mother who died in 1950. Mary, who died in 2000 aged ninety, was a midwife and is said to have delivered half the babies in the area. It was not uncommon for people to come up to her in the street as grown-ups thanking her for bringing them into the world.

After the war Lady Gabrielle continued nursing at Bystock and bicycled everywhere from Exeter to Exmouth. 'We used to go down to Exmouth to the cinema or whatever, and up on Woodbury Common where there was a marine camp. We were allowed to catch the marine bus to get back to the hospital. You could be the only woman on the bus and it was full of happy marines going back to camp and they couldn't have been better behaved. And if anybody swore, somebody would say "Ladies present."'

Lady Paulina went hunting with the Silverton and was a fearless rider. She had been given a horse, Claud, by my father, who was the Master and huntsman, a seventeen-hand black horse who hated men. 'I remember him chasing your father down the road with bared teeth,' she says.

In 1948, she had a 'coming-out' dance at Powderham. It was over the weekend of 6 to 8 August. Rose had had her coming-out just after the war. 'Rose had a dress made out

Nigel Knight Bruce with Lady Paulina Pepys on Claud, hacking to the meet in 1947. (Reproduced courtesy of the Solent News and Photo Agency.)

of curtain material and all the electricity failed,' says Lady Paulina.

'I only did half a Season,' recalls Lady Rose of the all-important social calendar for balls, cocktail parties and fashionable race meetings. 'It would have upset my mother if I hadn't done it. But I found myself crying and just getting even more of a social conscience.'

Food was scarce and the castle was subject to post-war rationing. 'It was endless macaroni cheese,' recalls Lady Paulina. It was also a time to cull the herd of fallow deer in the front park. 'I'm afraid several of them had their throats cut.'

There was no rationing for Timothy, however. 'We used to feed him strawberries and to a certain extent wisteria blossom,' she recalls. 'He was always there and we would take great joy in going to hunt for him.

'One day I went into the garden with our spaniel

Marker and we couldn't find Timothy. But the spaniel found him on his back where he had fallen down by the iris bed. He had fallen off the low wall but luckily the iris bed had broken his fall. Marker barked at him and I carried him safely back to the garden. Mallo had found him like this once too. '"E was peddling weth 'ees feet 'n th'air,' she told Lady Paulina. 'He was slow but he could certainly progress,' she remembers.

There were fancy-dress parties and evenings of charades. 'I remember your father dressed up as an Eastern potentate,' Lady Paulina told me, 'and he had to say, "Bring on the dancing girls", and clap his hands. Then he had to say, "Bring on Fatima", and an enormous but respectable colonel's wife appeared and ululated which we thoroughly enjoyed.' Parties would include all the local families, including the Fulfords of Great Fulford, the Studholmes of

The house party for Lady Paulina's coming-out dance.

Perridge, the Shelleys of Shobrooke Park and the Aclands of Feniton.

But for Paulina, Powderham had its constraints. 'It just seemed so narrow. It was the only life I had ever known. So when I went to Oxford, things just burst upon me.' It was here, while reading history, that she became interested in Russian Orthodoxy, joining the church in 1954 for twenty years. She has now returned to the Church of England.

Following the hotel enterprise, Lady Devon decided to open Powderham as a domestic science school. Originally, she had intended setting up a school for 'working-class girls' to be taught by old servants. 'Unfortunately, the old servants, whose great knowledge I wanted to pass on, were not very co-operative,' she concluded. The new school, with the 39-year-old Lady Devon as Principal, was intended instead for women who faced a future without domestic staff. Here girls could 'finish' without going to a finishing school abroad, which was difficult after the war with currency restrictions.

Powderham opened its doors and cleaning cupboards to twenty-five girls aged between sixteen and twenty-five in April 1947. The fees were seventy-five guineas a term and there would be a visit to Versailles to round off each year. Guest rooms were turned into small dormitories with pale primrose and green cretonnes.

'I want to take the terror out of housework,' said Lady Devon at the time. Little did she know what she had started when Mallo the French governess taught Lady Devon to cook. 'Cooking is an art which every girl should learn,' announced Lady Devon with a novice's enthusiasm. To this end, the girls were obliged to rise at 7.30 a.m., cook their own breakfasts, and not finish their day until they had washed up after dinner. It was a miracle that Timothy escaped a dusting.

Classes were given by three teachers in cooking, dress-making, laundry and housework. The old butler Clapton gave lessons in the care of silver, china and glassware and taught the girls how to choose the correct wines. Lord Devon took his hand in things and pronounced himself 'keen on home craft'.

The school attracted a great deal of wry amusement and press comment. But Lady Devon said, 'The girls' mothers are very pleased with the results we get. Although they do say their daughters are inclined to bully them when they get home because they don't approve of their "old-fashioned" methods of keeping house.'

However, the domestic science school was not a success. 'I think the castle was too big,' recalls Lady Paulina. 'My mother probably had more staff than she ought to have done.'

She remembers the girls giggling and laughing on the back stairs. They had got hold of the bust of the highly respectable 11th Earl and covered him in lipstick and eye shadow. 'It really was a few years before he got back to normal.'

'It was a way of getting the house clean,' says Lady Katherine Watney. 'The servants weren't going to come back. Young women from good families were going to have to do it themselves, so this is where they came to learn. They played sardines like people who knew the castle like the back of their hands.'

One of the girls was Lady Anne Coke, who later married Lord Glenconner. Together, they were pioneering

Lady Devon, principal of the domestic science school, holding Hugh's hand, talks to her pupils. (Reproduced courtesy of the Solent News and Photo Agency.)

residents of Mustique, where they entertained Princess Margaret and Mick Jagger, presumably to the highest standards of domestic hygiene.

Lady Katherine Watney recalls another exciting incident. 'There was a forest fire on Haldon which raged for days. It was started by a bottle being left in the sun near a picnic clearing given to the public by my godfather, Lord Mamhead. This was at Jackdaw Hill. I remember watching it from the castle. Rose got her first-aid kit out and went to help. So did the girls from the domestic science school who were very excited about getting some practical experience. Mummy just said, "I think everyone is overreacting."'

Rose then left and found her feet as a nurse in London. 'I fell in love with London. I was totally enthralled. My mother expected me to come home on my days off, but I just didn't want to. I worked at St Mary's, Paddington. I got to know the cockroaches very well. We had to work very hard and would have willingly gone without food. It was the "austerity food" of rationing, after all. I was a nurse for twenty years in the National Health Service. I did try private nursing but I found it very lonely. We went to the theatre, as we were given tickets. This was not to very good shows, or the ones we wanted to see, but it was fun.'

Lady Katherine Courtenay in her coming-out dress in 1958.

Lady Katherine was sent to school at Lawnside at Malvern. 'Mummy had me removed before I was expelled. I was talented in acting and speaking, and singing was my great gift. I can still give a good lead in church.' Hugh Courtenay went to Winchester, as his father did. When Timothy died, mention of it was made in the school magazine, *The Trusty Servant*.

The house opened to the public in 1960. 'My parents decided to open every day, after lunch. So from two to six people just took themselves round, although my parents were always in the garden or around the house to talk to them,' says Lady Katherine. 'I think the opening time was determined so that they could have their lunch undisturbed.'

There were plenty of things to look at for the historically minded: family portraits, the Music Room designed by the 3rd Earl before he was hounded into exile for his relationship with William Beckford, and the State Bedroom. Beyond the red ox-blood livery of the estate houses, at the Church of St Clement, holes can still be seen through which the Roundheads fired their muskets at the Royalist soldiers garrisoned at Powderham in the Civil War.

One day, after we had visited the church, I asked Lady Katherine if she would like to come sailing with me on the Exe estuary, on one of the small two-masted Topsham yawls which race there in the summer evenings. She replied politely with just one word: 'Vespers.'

Timothy took the opening of the castle to the public in his stride. No special fuss or attention was drawn to him by the guides. He just had the label put on him: 'My name is Timothy. I am very old. Please do not pick me up.'

The Devons loved showing people around, although the grant that paid for the new roof meant that Lord Devon had to give up his plumbing forays. Still, he would sit in the garden and chat to people.

Occasionally Lord Devon displayed the standards of his Victorian father. Asked to open the new swimming pool at Bickleigh in 1961, he agreed on condition the children all write an essay on Powderham Castle, which they had just visited.

'Wasn't this a bit harsh on seven- to eleven-year-olds?' a reporter from the *Daily Star* asked a spokesman for the castle. 'Not at all,' came the reply. 'I'm sure they enjoyed it.' Lord Devon offered to autograph the best essay.

Perhaps it was because they had read this that when, three years later, two men won (in a photographic competition) an invitation to have dinner with Lord Devon, they declined it. The option was dinner with the Earl and Countess or a postal order for ten pounds. 'We'd rather have the ten pounds,' S.R. Nice of Essex and R. Gibson of Bognor, Sussex, told the *Daily Mail* politely.

Lady Devon had an enduring love of horses and there were always plenty to see in the park, as Lady Katherine remembers. 'My mother was fixated with horses. Her father had let all his horses go to the Great War in 1916, including her horse Pilot Martin. She would have hidden him if she could. She was only nine. Thereafter, she would never part with any horses so we ended up with a park full of useless horses. If they were particularly useless she would breed from them, thereby perpetuating the problem.'

For Lady Gabrielle Courtenay there came a chance to exchange her bicycling trips into Exmouth for a journey to India and the North West Frontier to visit her sister Kathleen and her husband, Colonel Bill Birnie. 'I think I was meant to catch a husband there,' she says. 'But I didn't. I don't think I particularly wanted to. I was really happy and having so much fun at Powderham. It sounds so awful, but the British Raj was so wonderful to me, although I can't blame anyone for not wanting to be ruled by another country. I felt perfectly safe on the frontier and in Delhi I didn't have an escort or anything. I just behaved as if I was visiting London.'

There was a phrase for women who went out to India to find husbands but did not. They were called the 'returned empties'. But Lady Gabrielle did not return empty. She continued her fulfilling life of nursing, looking after her mother and living with her sister. She was content with her home, her family, her dogs and the tortoise. 'He was just there. That has been one of the most lovely things in life. If someone's just there.'

EIGHT

Changes at Powderham

'Nothing lasts in this world, at least without changing its physiognomy.'

Joseph Conrad, *Victory*

Just as Lady Gabrielle Courtenay enjoyed things 'just being there' at Powderham, so it was for the people who worked there. Few have more long-serving connections with the estate than Christine Manning and Gordon Mortimer. As indoor helper and tenant farmer, they represent two sides of the history of the place. Then there are the stories of the first administrator, Cedric Delforce, whose role would not have been out of place in Sir Alec Guinness's *Kind Hearts and Coronets*, and of Joy Maple, a castle guide, who had a secret and special affection for Timothy.

Christine Manning was the first person I met when beginning to write about Timothy. As I passed under the castle arch, she was opening the large wooden doors of the castle and sweeping the steps in preparation for the daily round of visitors, now about 40,000 a year.

Such visitor numbers were certainly not the case when Lieutenant Colonel Cedric Delforce, now eighty-six, came to Powderham in 1982 as the castle's administrator. He was sixty-five at the time.

The 17th Earl and Countess of Devon in their coronation robes in 1953.

'The situation was archaic. I came to introduce modernity,' says Cedric Delforce by telephone from his new home in Spain, where a fiesta with fireworks was going on. 'Of course, I didn't meet the tortoise a lot in the early days. I was far too busy looking at the accounts and answering to the trustees when there was a shortage of money,' he continues. 'There wasn't even a computer.'

The castle, he says, was not so much a tourist attraction as a private house that was open to the public. It was open from 2.30 to 5.30 p.m. from Monday to Thursday. One of the features for visitors was that the ladies were forbidden to wear stiletto heels in the castle. They were issued instead with slippers, which Cedric Delforce had got as a 'job lot' from Pan-American Airlines.

This amount of opening did not provide sufficient income, so the administrator had another idea. 'On Thursdays I gave guided tours myself at an extra charge, having been taught the family history by Lord and Lady Devon,' says Cedric Delforce. 'These were called "Connoisseur Days".

'Lord Devon would sit on the terrace and meet those members of the public and the children who were looking around. Of course Lord and Lady Devon fed Timothy every afternoon. Timothy was very much an attraction and many people came back each year and always asked after him.'

If Cedric wanted to speak to Lord Devon he would go and see his secretary. She in turn would rouse her master by means of an ancient speaking tube. 'The accounts were still being done on a bought ledger which was leather-bound,' he remembers.

Another triumph for Cedric Delforce was attracting the Devon motor show to the grounds and the first product launch at the castle. The Daimler Sovereign was unveiled there, against the backdrop of the turrets and Timothy's Rose Garden, although Timothy was somehow obscured from the final advertisements.

At seventy, Cedric Delforce asked if he could retire, but that is not the way of things at Powderham. He went on as administrator until he was seventy-two, before being switched to a part-time role in the vaults of the family archives. 'Lord Devon also asked me if I would look after his private affairs, which I did.' Finally, at the age of eighty-two, he was allowed to retire.

'I got on extremely well with Lady Devon. She had very high standards, although she could be domineering, some would say bossy. But she had spent a lot of time emptying buckets when the roof still leaked and was determined to make the castle work.'

The roof is a recurring theme of both pride and worry among the family and the estate. Cedric Delforce remembers the Ministry of Works craftsmen coming down. They had just re-roofed Hampton Court Palace in London. 'They were real craftsmen,' he says. 'They did it and admired it with great pride.'

Cedric Delforce is credited with opening the first gift shop. 'It wasn't commercial or anything like that,' he remembers. Lady Devon took particular pride in selecting the various 'gifts' which would be available. It won an award from *Which?* magazine for the best-value gift shop in a small house.

'Hugh Courtenay, as he then was, was a real countryman. He wasn't interested in the house. He was much more concerned with protecting wildlife habitats. In particular, I remember him getting a wildlife site at Exminster protected so that it could not be built upon.'

It was at about this time that Powderham opened for cross-country events and Princess Anne came to stay. There is also a letter in the archives from the Queen Mother asking Lady Devon to advise her on a pony for Princess Elizabeth.

Perhaps Cedric Delforce's greatest service to Lord Devon, however, was to establish the Courtenay Society. 'People kept writing to Lord Devon from all over the world asking about their family history and the Courtenay name,' he remembers. It is thanks to him, given Lord

Devon's fascination with unopened envelopes, that they ever got a reply.

For Christine Manning, the estate that brought her the greatest happiness in her life, and that of her uncle and grandfather, also brought a day of great sadness. This was 15 September 1987, when Lord Devon sold his herd of South Devon cattle, which he had started in 1948.

'It broke my heart,' says Christine Manning. 'They are the gentle giants of beef and I had worked with them since 1972.' The catalogue for the dispersal sale carries a photograph of 'Powderham Gem 9th' (South Devon 'Bull of the Year' 1979) and he looks a particularly fine specimen. All the cattle were named after precious or semi-precious stones.

The sale made nearly £100,000 but, as Lord Courtenay pointed out at the time to the *Western Morning News*, 'The herd was too small to fit into the present big farming business.' He also told the paper that he was now farming 1,500 acres 'in hand' compared with only twenty-six acres forty years previously when the estate was farmed mainly by tenant farmers.

The sale was another example of the unpredictable troughs of West Country farming. The cost of grain had risen so steeply that to rear a double-suckling herd on this scale became uneconomic.

Now seventy, Christine Manning explains that her family have worked at Powderham for more than 150 years. 'Two generations of my family worked at Powderham before me: first my grandfather, and then my uncle, who was succeeded as house carpenter by my father, George Hitchcock. Even my sister Joyce worked briefly as a nurserymaid to the present Lord Devon, while my brother,

Gerald, still cares for the restoration of the estate's antiques.'

Christine was born in 1933 at the heart of the estate in a house in Kenton's 'South Town', next door to Marsh Farm, the 'Home Farm'. The cart horses used for the timber wagons were kept at Marsh Farm, and as a small child she used to bed them down with dried bracken. The grooms would put a ladder up against them so that she and her brothers could climb up on board and brush them.

'My earliest memory of the Courtenays was quite simply that they were always there,' she says. 'I first saw the present earl at a village fête when he was six or seven, wearing a Norfolk jacket and a cap. I felt sorry because he looked so utterly lost.'

She looked after the horses, and then the herd of Devon cattle. When she married, the Devons offered her a cottage for £250. 'By the time we actually came to buy it, they insisted we paid only a hundred and fifty,' she remembers. 'We named it "Merrivay", after a book I had read where they put a fir tree on the completed house, which builders used to do.'

When Lady Katherine married in 1966 she asked Christine to help her to dress for the wedding at Kenton church. She was there for Hugh, Lord Courtenay's twenty-first birthday party for the villagers. 'I can remember the laughter now when he rode around the Music Room on a pony.

'When my father was close to death in 1964, he held on to his last breath until Lord Devon arrived. Lady Devon wrote my father's obituary and it came straight from the heart.'

After the cattle were sold in 1987, Christine Manning worked for the late Lord and Lady Devon. 'Lady Devon used to call me her "other daughter".'

Outside a pretty cottage and garden overlooking a field of ripening corn towards the Exe estuary, a man is sitting on a bench, drinking a mug of tea and smoking a pipe. The square tower of Exmouth's Trinity Church beyond is bathed in sunshine.

This is a moment of reflection on a sunny day for Gordon Mortimer, now eighty, whose family have been tenant farmers at Powderham since 1790. He drinks his tea from a mug which says 'His Lordship' and he is clearly the master of all he surveys, a brilliant orange red-hot poker flaming at his side.

He was born on Christmas Day 1923, at Exwell Barton, and is the seventh generation of Mortimers to have lived there. 'My great-grandfather just rode over the hills here and fell in love with the place. He asked for and got a farm from the Courtenays.'

Exwell is a 700-acre farm stretching down to the marsh ground of the Exe where waders, cormorants and sea divers come up from the river for shelter. 'I used to keep the marshes free of sedge and rushes,' says Gordon who took over from his father in 1950. His son Charles, now fifty-one, has taken over from him. There he would graze 300 Devon and South Devon cattle, and the horses used for pulling the barges and ships up the nearby Exeter Ship Canal.

'The cart horses used to guide boats up the canal and then we would rest them on the marshes,' he remembers. 'They were stabled upstream at the Turf, which is now a pub. The stables are the beer cellars.'

Today the marshes have grown up, although they still sustain a few head of cattle. 'It is a wicked shame really,' says Gordon. 'They have been let go because of flooding.'

Gordon Mortimer was too busy farming to pay much heed to Timothy. 'I did meet him twice, but my wife and children visited him often. I could not have said that sentence to you a year ago,' he continues, his eyes looking into the middle distance. He was recently widowed.

Although his father suffered a heart attack in middle age, he lived to be ninety-eight. His mother was ninety-one and they were married for sixty years. This is yet another instance of longevity in this settled community and among those who knew Timothy.

There have been many changes. The horses no longer pull the ships up the canal, and shipping traffic itself has all but gone. There was such excitement on the farm when Gordon's father brought home the first crawler tractor in the West Country in 1947. Now large Fords and John Deere tractors speed the plough and along the lanes.

In 1950, £12 paid for eight men to work on the farm each week. Today that figure is £300 for one man alone.

They used to have a saying, Gordon tells me, based on the leaves of the trees, which would determine the weather for the summer:

> Oak before ash, only a little splash.
> Ash before the oak, summer soak.

This year, the oak was out a long time before the ash, which Gordon predicts will bring a fine summer.

I am able to return to him a little bit of country lore

which I have just learned and he has never heard. We are talking about cuckoos, as he had seen his first swallow and heard his first cuckoo this year on the same day.

'Turn a coin over in your pocket when you hear your first cuckoo and you will be prosperous,' I tell him. 'Well, I'm damned,' he replies in a Devon expression of amazement.

'I don't want to see things altered, but they have changed,' continues Gordon, who had only left Devon twice before he was sixty-five. He remembers that in the 1950s there were twenty tenant farmers at Powderham, and they would always have a Michaelmas Rent Dinner at the Devon Arms, hosted by the Courtenay family. 'These were big occasions,' he recalls. Today there are only two tenant farmers on the estate.

Gordon Mortimer can vividly recall the farm being covered with paper during the war, after a bomb had hit St Loye's College in Exeter. 'It fluttered down on the land but as soon as you touched it, disintegrated. It had travelled four miles.' He also recalls being out farming one day and seeing dark shadows on the estuary. 'We didn't know what they were and were told not to ask.' They were the 'Mulberry Harbour' concrete barges used for the D-Day landings.

In the winter of 1963, even in its warm microclimate, Powderham froze to a standstill. 'I know I shouldn't have done, but I took my wife, children and four dogs out on to the Exe, which had completely frozen over,' says Gordon, enjoying the sunshine, his pipe and the memory. 'When we were in the middle, it began to crack like rifle shots. We packed together and then spread out, eventually making it back to the shore.' When the ice began to melt, it banked up on the shoreline to a height of twenty feet.

One incident has remained with Gordon Mortimer all his life. One day he met a French onion seller, Jean-Pierre from Roscoff, who needed help getting his boat up the canal, and they became friends. Then the son of Jean-Pierre came over to Exeter and disappeared.

'I would see his father looking for him everywhere with a forlorn face,' recalls Gordon Mortimer. 'He came back year after year to look for him, but he was never found.'

If Gordon Mortimer only left Devon twice in his first sixty-five years, he certainly made up for it in his retirement, when he moved from the farm to Verbena Cottage, where he now lives. With his wife Freda he went round the world several times. They had trips to China, the Amazon, South Africa and the Seychelles. 'I saw a big tortoise there,' he says. In Cape Town he asked the taxi driver to stop as a giant tortoise crossed the road. 'He gave him a whole peach and I watched as it ate the lot in moments,' remembers Gordon.

Gordon's wife, who made prayer mats for the church, always wanted to go to Bora Bora in the South Pacific. 'It was her dream to feed the fishes,' says Gordon. 'She loved that day and died three weeks after we got back.'

'The estate today is really pulled round,' admits Gordon Mortimer. When they hold concerts there, he is often to be found going round with a bucket collecting for the church. This normally raises about £3,000. He was also involved in raising money for the Penlee lifeboat disaster of 1981, which claimed the lives of eight lifeboat men.

To socialise now, Gordon Mortimer goes to the nearby Starcross Sailing and Cruising Club, affectionately known as 'the Boozers and Cruisers Club'. He started it in 1949 with eight friends and they have premises built by Brunel, of the same Devon red stone used for his railway. Gordon is the President and for his eightieth birthday the members gave him a 'Certificate of Entitlement' to a year's free beer. 'I do have my own tankard, but I don't often drink more than a pint,' he says. The estate also gave him a birthday party on Christmas Day.

Instead of socialising at the club, though, he prefers the bench outside the back of his cottage, where the open door to the tool shed tells its own story. 'My swallows always come in the third week of April and nest here. I leave the door open for them.'

For seventeen years, Gordon Mortimer had a sheep dog called Bob who lived in the shed. 'He didn't mind them and I would always ask him, "Where are your swallows, Bob?"' The sheep dog is gone now, but the door remains open.

Being a guide today at Powderham is a long way from Cedric Delforce's 'Connoisseur Days'. 'I suppose it's become more commercial?' he asked when we spoke on the telephone as another Spanish firecracker exploded down the line. The answer is that visitors are still guided around, with as much knowledge and affection, by people such as Joy Maple, who paid special attention to Timothy.

'A year ago, Timothy became poorly with a calcium build-up. He couldn't feed himself properly. He liked lettuce, cucumber and tomato, anything with a bit of water in it.'

Every day after her morning guided tour, Joy would skin a grape for Timothy, giving him half at a time. 'I just used to think he was a lovely little character, a charming, basic creature. He had tiny, pinprick eyes, but he could give you such a look.

'Last summer, when it was very warm, he was marvellous. He would come across the lawn to me for his food. Then, in the cold weather, he didn't want to move at all. Sometimes he would snatch a lettuce leaf from my hand, which he could give a nip. He would also nip my toes when I wore sandals.'

Joy had a child's watering can and used to spray him gently. 'I cooled him with it in a flat plant saucer when it was hot. I called that his swimming pool.'

NINE

Lives in the Balance: The fate of other tortoises

I do remember an apothecary, –
And hereabouts he dwells, – which late I noted
In tatter'd weeds, with overwhelming brows,
Culling of simples; meager were his looks,
Sharp misery had worn him to the bones:
And in his needy shop a tortoise hung,
An alligator stuff'd, and other skins
Of ill-shaped fishes; and about his shelves
A beggarly account of empty boxes,
Green earthen pots, bladders, and musty seeds,
Remnants of packthread, and old cakes of roses,
Were thinly scatter'd, to make up a show.

William Shakespeare, *Romeo and Juliet*: the description of the apothecary's shop where Romeo bought the poison with which he killed himself

Just as Gilbert White's tortoise was measured, amid much amusement, on the grocer's scales at Selborne, so too was Timothy at Powderham. White's tortoise, which had weighed 'six pounds 9 ounces: & 1/2 averdupoise'* in

* Averdupoise, now spelt avoirdupois, is a system of weights based on a pound of sixteen ounces, equal to 7000 grains (0.4536 kilogrammes).

October 1779, weighed 'after a fast of 7, or 8, months, only 6 pounds 4 ounces'.

Writing this entry in his diary on 17 May 1780, Gilbert White continues: 'Timothy begins to break his fast May 13th on the globe-thistle and American willow-herb; his favourite food is lettuce, & dandelion, cucumber, & kidney-beans.'

At Powderham Timothy was weighed by David Spratt in 1990 and again by his father-in-law Brian Chapman in 1995. David Spratt, fifty-five, had earlier been involved, with his wife Christine, in measuring giant tortoises in the Seychelles and giant and small tortoises throughout the UK. They live at Shell Park near Tavistock in Devon. An emblem of a tortoise is at the top of their writing paper.

'I went down myself and met Timothy,' says David Spratt, a biomedical scientist and zoologist. The results of his weighing of Timothy were published in *The Veterinary Record* under the heading 'Jackson's Ratio Revisited'. The ratio tells you if the tortoise is the right weight for its length. It was devised in 1976 by the late Dr Oliphant Jackson, as a means of checking the health of the smaller species of tortoises, and is explained as follows:

> *Introduction*
>
> In 1976 the late Dr Oliphant Jackson, MRCVS, recorded the weights and measurements of a large number of healthy and sick Mediterranean tortoises, both *Testudo græca* (spur-thighed tortoise) and *T. hermanni* (Hermann's tortoise). He observed that in healthy tortoises there is an optimum body weight, which can be used as one of the criteria to assess the state of health of these species and their suitability for hibernation.

If the figures for the average weights are plotted on a graph they provide a very useful guideline. The data can also be calculated as a weight/length ratio, now known as the 'Jackson Ratio'; but for practical purposes, Dr Jackson recommended using the graph, which also shows the lower weight limits of healthy tortoises.

How to assess your tortoise

To make use of the graph, you must take your measurements in metric units (millimetres and grammes). The carapace is measured in a straight line, which can be achieved by pressing the front of the shell against a vertical surface to push the head right in, and pressing another vertical surface against the tail end. Measure the distance between these two points in millimetres. The weight (in grammes) can be found using an accurate pair of kitchen scales, or for smaller specimens you may need a balance or electronic scales.

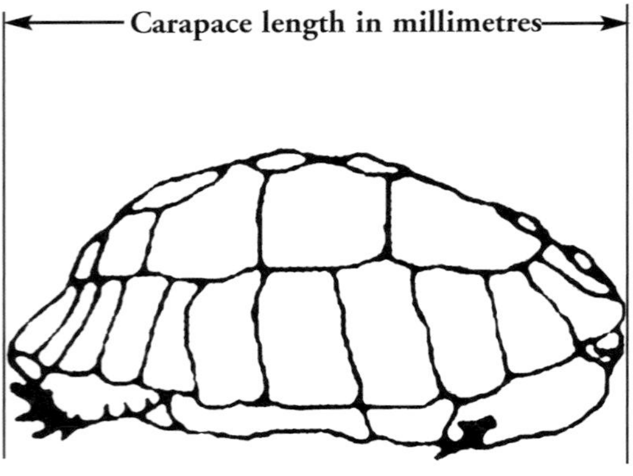

The carapace length of a tortoise is measured in a straight line

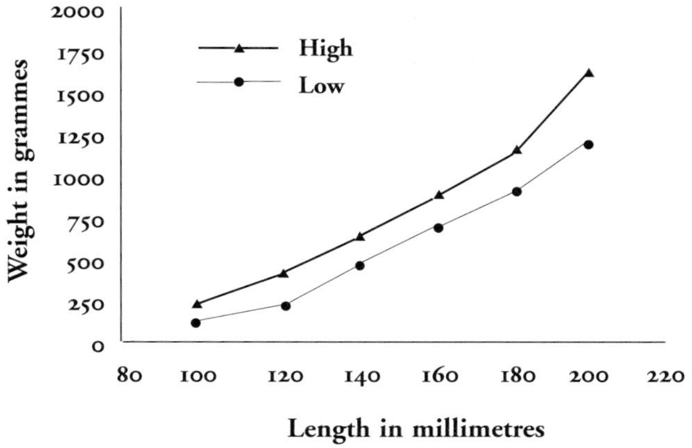

Now use your data to find a point on the chart: draw a vertical line on the graph corresponding to your tortoise's length, and a horizontal line across from its weight. Mark the spot where the lines meet, and you can then see if it falls within the range for healthy tortoises.

How to interpret your findings

When weighing, there are several points to bear in mind. Firstly, a tortoise that has just emptied its bladder of 50ml of water will be 50 grammes lighter, and conversely it will be heavier after a drink. Secondly, a female carrying eggs will be deceptively heavy, even if not eating.

Thirdly, an overweight tortoise may be full of body fat or fluid, and is not necessarily healthy. If there are no apparent problems with your tortoise, and its weight falls within the healthy range on the graph, you can safely assume that it can be hibernated.

However, if it falls into the 'dangerously low' category, veterinary attention should be sought, and the animal should be overwintered until its weight is restored. Many tortoises which die in hibernation simply have insufficient body reserves to see them through the winter. Similarly a grossly overweight tortoise should have a veterinary check-up to investigate possible abnormal causes.

A tortoise that is still growing may increase its length by up to 2mm in a good summer, with a corresponding increase in weight. It is recommended that tortoises are weighed at least once a month as a more reliable guide. Regular weighing will give you an early indication of any adverse trend and alert you to the possible need for veterinary treatment.

'Timothy was a fine specimen,' recalls David Spratt. 'I was able to weigh him, but I could not accurately age him from looking at his carapace.'

These were his findings:

Allometric* equation for calculating length from body weight is: $L = 17.5(W)^{0345}$. This formula was derived from data collected from surveys carried out in the Republic of the Seychelles in 1986 of free-ranging and captive giant tortoises, and the UK in 1989–90 of captive giant tortoises and captive smaller tortoises of a number of species.

Timothy: 13 May 1990:
Straight length = 25.8cm
Straight width = 19.2cm
Curved length = 31.3cm
Curved width = 33.2cm
Weight = 3kg
Calculated length for weight = 25.56cm

*Allometry is the ratio between two sizes or weights.

Timothy: 5 September 1995:
Straight length = 25.7cm
Straight width = 17.78cm
Curved length = 31.75cm
Curved width = 30.5cm
Weight = 4.08kg
Calculated length for weight = 28.43cm

Conclusion: Timothy is slightly overweight, but would be putting on weight through the summer in preparation for hibernation.

David Spratt wrote to Tim Faulkner, general manager of Powderham, after the two visits, with the following observations:

> Although there appear to be strange anomalies between some measurements, these need not bother us since the anatomical criteria for reference points from which to take measurements are subject to a degree of interpretation. The differences you see are understandable.
>
> Tortoises will grow throughout life but annual changes in body dimensions will become very small in an animal of Timothy's age. This can be seen dramatically in the giants, where there is a surge of growth up to about forty or fifty years of age and then this may slow to a crawl for the rest of their lives.
>
> The interesting finding at this weighing (1995) is the 37 per cent increase in Timothy's bodyweight. Using the formula in my paper, his length in 1990 should have been 25.56cm (actual was 25.8cm). For an animal of his weight this year (1995) he should ideally be 28.43cm long (actual was 25.7cm).

This is no cause for concern, probably the opposite, but I would be interested to know if he has had a change of diet, or his habits have changed.

Tim Faulkner replied: 'Timothy does his own thing and remains outside, as he always has done, burying himself in a deep pile of leaves. Last year he did not hibernate until late December and was back out in early March.'

David Spratt then suggested that someone should be allowed to weigh Timothy each week. 'This may encourage other tortoise owners to pay closer attention to their own animals, a small promotion for animal welfare,' he wrote. His proposal was not taken up, for which the tortoise might have felt some relief. Tim Faulkner was concerned that a weekly weighing might attract too much publicity, which might result in a theft of Timothy. 'We are always looking at ways of making him safer from this threat, which seems beyond our alarm suppliers.'

David Spratt was also able to make other useful observations about Timothy and tortoises in general. He points out that the underside of the tortoise is called a plastron, which in males tends to be concave. 'The reason for this is so that when the male mounts the female, he will not roll off. Her carapace will fit into his plastron.' This is noteworthy when one recalls Gilbert White remarking that a tortoise may spend a whole month in a single act of copulation.

Then there are breeding considerations which determine the different shell shapes, says David Spratt. 'The female has a flat plastron, so she builds a nest like a sock, lands the eggs at the bottom, covers it with soil and flattens it down in a single movement.'

David Spratt points out that the structure of the carapace is thick bone, covered in six-sided scutes composed of keratin. In between the scutes is a softer tissue containing nerves which are as sensitive as a human fingernail bed.

He disputes the belief that the age of a tortoise may be accurately determined after death by counting the rings on the scutes, like measuring the age of a felled oak tree by its interior rings. 'The tortoise rings can be aged and measured externally,' he says, 'but what actually happens is that as each scute grows the earlier scutes tend to disappear and blend into the keratin. Also, the laying down of rings year on year will depend very much on environmental conditions and food. In a good year they may grow rings, in a bad year they will not.'

So we are left none the wiser as to Timothy's exact age. But having studied him with his expert eye, David Spratt concludes: 'The record of his age seems pretty sound.'

It may be considered something of a miracle that Timothy was never stolen, given that he was left alone with members of the public in the garden for hours on end. But the fates, like those who looked after him, were kind.

His was a life in stark contrast to those of many of the thousands of tortoises who were used as food on ships or who entered Britain to be sold as pets, and whose fate eventually resulted in a total ban on the importation of tortoises in 1984. 'In earlier times, they were stacked alive in ships as meat for the crew,' explains David Spratt. 'They were stored upside down to prevent movement and required very little food or water to survive. They were stored randomly and killed as required for fresh meat.'

The statistics on importation speak for themselves and

Lady Katherine Watney feeding Timothy, circa 1969.

the Herpetological Society (who undertake the study of frogs and reptiles), the Tortoise Trust and DEFRA, the government agency, have much information on the fate of tortoises. In short, this information contrasts sharply with the innocent notion of having a tortoise in the garden and makes Timothy's achievement of longevity all the more remarkable.

According to DEFRA:

- Between 1969 and 1972, 480,000 spur-thighed tortoises were imported to Britain.
- Between 1976 and 1979, nearly one million Horsfield tortoises were exported from the wild and three quarters of these, an average of 30,000 a year, were exported to Europe.
- Since 1996, more than 15,000 tortoises have been imported to Europe from outside the EU.

The first recorded commercial importation of tortoises into Britain (the arrival of Gilbert White's tortoise at Chichester was part of a simple mariner's custom) appears in 1886 in Norfolk. Sir Peter Eade bought some tortoises from a street trader in Norwich and detailed their habits in a local zoological journal.

By the 1920s, hundreds of thousands of tortoises were being imported. In the years after the Second World War 300,000 entered Britain from Morocco. Others managed to get in from Algeria, Tunisia and Libya.

In 1964, the UK Animals (Restriction of Import) Act was passed, requiring the number of tortoises imported to be registered. By 1976 this number had exceeded two million, according to the Tortoise Trust. It is hard to imagine where they all went, although it is accepted elsewhere in Europe that a significant number went to making soup in such culinary fleshpots as Marseilles.

Even as late as 1980, live tortoises could be bought in French fishmongers. In 1979 an application was made for the importation of 700,000 tortoises to France. This was stopped only because a survey was done on fifty-six *Testudo græca* imported to France from the backstreets of Tangiers and they were found to contain traces of the salmonella organism. Given their provenance, it's a wonder that's all they had.

In 1969, a report now with the Tortoise Trust detailed the collection of tortoises, mainly *Testudo græca* like Timothy, in Casablanca. 'They are mostly brought in by shepherds with their animals each week on market day. They are then sent in sacks, in vans or on top of public buses to the port. They are stowed upright on deck. The seamen, with uncertain humanity, spray the baskets with seawater to prevent the creatures from roasting in the sun. In this way between 10,000 and 25,000 tortoises are despatched to London once a fortnight.' Gilbert White, in 1773, noted that his tortoise disliked direct sunlight. 'Though he loves warm weather he avoids the hot sun; because his thick shell, when once heated, would as the poets say of solid armour – "scald with safety".'

If a tortoise died before its journey to England, its carapace would often be turned into a banjo for sale as a curio for tourists. An incident was recorded in 1952 in Morocco in which a group of street boys came upon a barrel of tortoises and hurled bricks at them, stoning them to death.

Tortoises were killed both by cruelty and kindness. The Moroccans placed a low value upon them and English households misunderstood how they would cope with the change in climate. It was accepted, however, that the practice of trying to imitate the sandy climate of Casablanca by putting tortoises in airing cupboards merely led to suffocation.

In 1987 a four-year survey was undertaken upon 606 tortoises in England purchased as pets. By the end of the study, 404 had died in hibernation and another 137 had perished from other causes, which might have included being brought indoors to hibernate. A further 57 had died from inanition or dullness.

There is a difference between leaving a tortoise out and turning him out. In 1983, 250 tortoises were found abandoned by a dealer in a London street. This provoked questions in Parliament about the restriction of imports.

The irony is that now, with global warming, tree felling in South American rainforests and CFCs causing holes in the ozone layer, the English climate is much milder than it used to be and more suited to keeping tortoises. But it is still the statistical contention of the Tortoise Trust that few tortoises survive the first winter of their hibernation.

There is on the Seychelles a tortoise called Esmeralda. She is more than 150 years old. It is thought that she was being held for food on the *Hirondelle* when the ship went down off Bird Island and she escaped. There are two coincidences here. One is that the ship's name means swallow and tortoises in England come out of hibernation with the arrival of the swallows in spring; the other is that just as Timothy was found to be of the opposite sex, Esmeralda was found to be a male. Her name has not been changed.

On the Galapagos today, much is made of a giant tortoise called 'Lonesome' George. He stands in age and interest above the other wildlife there, although the alleged, hushed-up finding of the remains of a female mate does not support the idea that scientists moved him from one island to another.

The records of Tomas de Berlanga, Bishop of Panama in 1535, show that tortoises were a feature of the Galapagos even then. The bishop and his ship were becalmed on their journey from Panama to Peru when they sighted the Galapagos Islands. Losing two men and ten horses in their search for water, they ended up eating cactus pads for moisture. The bishop relayed his findings of tortoises, sea lions and iguanas to his emperor, Carlos V of Spain, who had the Flemish cartographer Abraham Ortelius include the islands in his *Orbis Terrarum* of 1574. There is no mention of turtles. The islands are clearly designated in Spanish as 'Insulae de los Galopegos,' meaning 'Tortoise Islands'.

But even dry land, sanctuary in England and the

warmth of a palace garden were no guarantee that a tortoise would survive. In 1628, William Laud, Archbishop of Canterbury, brought a tortoise to Lambeth Palace in London. The tortoise outlived the archbishop's impeachment by the Long Parliament (Laud was a Royalist) in 1640 and execution in 1645. Having survived until 1750, the tortoise was accidentally killed by a gardener's fork. His carapace remains at Lambeth Palace today.

The legacy of Laud and his tortoise lives on in Oxford. In 1631, Laud commissioned the Canterbury Quad at Christ Church and, to celebrate this event, there began tortoise racing. The Oxford colleges still hold annual tortoise races, to which a recent report from Regent's Park College bears witness:

> Regent's racing tortoise, Emmanuelle, for many years proved to be the fastest tortoise in Oxford at the inter-collegiate tortoise fairs, has now been overtaken. Fortunately, the younger supplanter is also a Regent's tortoise, named less magnificently as 'Fred'. 'Fred' won by a long head from the St John's tortoise at the race in Trinity Term, an event conducted under the strictest rules of animal welfare and with the greatest respect for tortoises.

Ten

Music Comes to Powderham

'Like most dreamers, to whom it is given sometimes to hear the music of the spheres, Heyst, the wanderer of the Archipelago, had a taste for silence which he had been able to gratify for years.'

Joseph Conrad, *Victory*

It cannot be said for certain that tortoises like music, and for years at Powderham Timothy had been exposed to little more than the soft zephyrs of the occasional string quartet. When family plays had been put on at Leslie House, outside the lodge gates of the Kenton drive, he had sometimes been taken there to enjoy the spectacle from the safety of a shrub bed on the lawn.

But nothing was to prepare him for the arrival of top pop bands, which started appearing at Powderham in the 1990s. Not only did the artistes congregate on the lawn of the Rose Garden, but the performances took place just below, often with fireworks and 10,000 spectators, at the spot where Timothy had fallen into the iris bed.

The advent of these concerts was the brainwave of general manager Tim Faulkner, now forty-three. As an officer in the Life Guards he had run the musical rides for the

Household Cavalry. 'I got into outside events,' he says. He was appointed to Powderham in 1992, having been encouraged to apply by a regimental friend, Andrew Parker-Bowles. He had been brought up on a farm in Sussex and his wife Charlotte was the daughter of the farm next door.

Faulkner's father had been secretary of the Belvoir hunt but had died young at fifty-eight while out hunting when his son was with him. His last words as he died in Long Clawson Lane, with the hounds disappearing in full cry, were: 'I think they'll soon be in Quorn country.'

With their farming and country background, the Faulkners were drawn to Powderham and rented a small house at Starcross. After two years following the Caribbean trade winds on their twenty-seven-foot yacht, it was time to settle down.

Visitor numbers at Powderham were down to 12,000 a year and, says Tim Faulkner, the atmosphere was sleepy. 'It was a beautiful place, but rather shabby. It was clear the family had just done everything themselves and I was faced with a moribund organization.'

The record attendance at the castle for visitors had been 60,000 in 1974. The attraction was the display of Princess Anne's wedding dress. She had taken part in the Powderham Horse Trials, and Hugh Courtenay had been at Cambridge University with their mutual friend, the international show jumper Richard Meade. But twenty years later it was obvious that it would take more than a royal bridal gown to compete for the attentions of holiday makers in the West Country. So Tim Faulkner decided to concentrate on entertainment for Devonians as well.

'You won't last – they never do,' an old castle maintenance man, Ted Dunn, had told him. Such people felt they owned the castle and didn't want change.

'I was at the level where if a room needed painting or a loo needed cleaning, I would do it,' says Tim Faulkner. And he was determined to last.

Faulkner set about recruiting Exeter University students as guides. 'They were bright and attractive and I knew we were on to a winner.' In 1992, there was a core group of ten people looking after the castle opening. Today there are the equivalent of ninety full-time jobs. 'We have as many employees as the estate ever had in its hey-day,' says Faulkner.

But it was an article from a 1963 back issue of *Country Life* that first brought a sprinkle of modernity and glamour to the castle. The castle had been spotted by location finder Joe Friedman, who was looking for somewhere to shoot Kazuo Ishiguro's Booker prize-winning novel *The*

Party to celebrate the 17th Earl of Devon's 80th birthday and his grandson Charlie Courtenay's 21st in 1997.

Remains of the Day, with Merchant Ivory. James Ivory came to look round the castle but gave no reaction until he came to the grand staircase, a faded sweep of oak floorboards and peeling turquoise paint, lit only by a white boxed cupola in the roof. 'I could tell from his reaction that this was the moment he was serious,' says Faulkner. 'He said it was fantastic.'

There followed a discussion about how much it would cost to rent Powderham for a set number of filming days and the company offered £37,000 for fourteen days. Neither Devonians nor film companies like being tied down too precisely to time, so Faulkner replied: 'Why don't you have the castle for as long as you like for £50,000,' and an agreement was struck. In the end, they filmed for seventeen days.

Starring in the film were Emma Thompson, Sir Anthony Hopkins, Edward Fox, Hugh Grant, Christopher Reeve and Lady Devon's lead-crystal brandy glasses. 'The props people came rushing through from the Music Room one day saying the ones they had were of such poor quality, and could I help?' says Diana Devon (who became Countess of Devon on the death of her father-in-law in 1998, when Hugh Courtenay became the 18th Earl).

'You know how we live here in the middle bit,' says Lady Devon as we sit chatting informally, while Cheetah the lurcher jumps on to my lap. The crew filmed in the state rooms, which are rarely used by the family.

Although she is High Sheriff of Devon and her husband Hugh is Vice Lord Lieutenant of the county, the atmosphere is one of relaxation in their own private part of the castle – it's dogs on the sofa. Not ten strides away from where we are sitting, a door goes out into the Rose Garden where Timothy lived.

'I was just name-dropping a bit,' says Diana Devon as her husband comes through having been exercising the shooting spaniels. 'The star most likely to have met Timothy was a chap called Christopher Reeve,' she thinks. The *Superman* star used to go riding in the park strictly against the insurance policy of the film-makers, Merchant Ivory.

She remembers meeting him for the first time and thinking, Who the hell is Christopher Reeve? 'And I obviously gave that look on my face, but thank God he never saw it. We actually became great mates, because 'Superman' was very into his riding and we had a spare horse at the time.'

Was Superman any good at riding? 'I'm afraid what eventually happened to him does not surprise me at all,' says Diana Devon with her customary honesty, referring to the accident that left him paralysed from the neck down. 'We'd go and have these jumping sessions and he used to come to a fence and start going, "Help, help, I can't see the stride." Once he did exactly what he did when he broke his neck. He went to jump and the horse took an extra stride and he went straight over its head. He was very good about that.'

Lord Devon, who like his wife has ridden and hunted since he was a child, remembers him as well: 'I'm afraid he had a loose seat and there was nothing natural about his riding, as if he had just been taught in the sandpit of a riding school.'

'But he did meet Timothy, although I can't remember when,' continues Diana Devon. Sadly, Emma Thompson did not. She looked him up in the diary she always keeps when filming. 'I am afraid there is no entry for the tortoise,' came the reply. Perhaps she was preoccupied. 'She used to greet me each morning with a kiss,' says Tim Faulkner.

Sir Anthony Hopkins, who had just made *The Silence of the Lambs*, was more interested in Peggy, the almost stone-deaf daily. They would sit in the garden together sharing Kit-Kats. 'She has been here for ever,' says Lady Devon. 'Almost as long as Timothy. And she was always around for him, doing her polishing and dusting.'

The actors stayed at the Royal Clarence Hotel in Exeter and came to the set each day at Powderham in chauffeur-driven cars. On the last day, Hopkins left, then stopped his driver and made him return to the castle. 'He came running through the house shouting, "Where's Peggy, I haven't said goodbye to Peggy,"' recalls Diana Devon. 'Do you know, he ran all the way through the house, found Peggy and signed an autograph on a picture of himself "with love to Peggy and thanks for looking after us". It was a great gift – amazing really.'

'The castle benefited,' says Tim Faulkner of the filming. 'Visitor figures were up 30 per cent and we all went to the première in Exeter *en masse*.'

But it was the summer concerts and picnics that really started to take off. Starting gently with the Midland Symphony Orchestra in 1993 and 3,000 people, there followed Sarah Brightman, Michael Ball with his show tunes, and in the late 1990s, Chris de Burgh, who attracted 10,000 people. 'He came into the Rose Garden after the concert and, from what I can remember of it, Timothy was kept up till well after two in the morning,' says Tim Faulkner.

This was an early high spot, hinting of things to come: later Roger Daltrey of The Who and Gary Brooker of Procol Harum visited the Rose Garden for drinks before they went on stage.

Did Timothy turn a whiter shade of pale or 'Skip the Light Fandango'? Tim Faulkner remembers sitting with Gary Brooker, talking about shooting, when there were countless calls for Brooker to go on stage. He just carried on chatting and finished his drink before leisurely walking down the garden. Perhaps he thought Timothy would 'turn a cartwheel cross the floor'.

Slightly more alarming for Timothy was the arrival of Status Quo, with whose lead guitarist Rick Parfitt I once spent an interesting day in a helicopter visiting children's hospitals in Edinburgh. He just managed not to fall out. Fortunately Timothy and Lady Gabrielle Courtenay made themselves scarce when he played. Status Quo photographed the cover pictures for their album *Riff* at Powderham, and perhaps because they were mindful of his safety and hearing, Timothy does not appear in them.

One of the features of a Status Quo concert is that people insist on standing up and doing a dance which looks as if a builder is stretching his braces. At the Reading Festival in 1973, those of us at the back had an answer for this (which reminds me of the little boy at the Elms peeing on my foot). We would 'go' into our empty lager cans and simply hurl them towards the front. It worked every time, especially among those who thought they were getting free beer. So far as I know, this practice has not been taken up at Powderham yet.

There is a story at Powderham that Timothy took

exception to Sir Elton John. 'The truth is, they never met,' says Tim Faulkner. 'It had nothing to do with him playing "Crocodile Rock".'

But it was the year when The Who's Roger Daltrey played that put Timothy in most danger. Faulkner had decided to have fireworks in the Rose Garden, with rivers of fire pouring like molten lead off the castle roof.

'I admit I did have my reservations when they all started going off and the castle seemed ablaze,' says Faulkner. 'I was concerned for Timothy and the house. It was like World War Three … but Timothy, having survived the Blitz, took it like a trooper.'

When he was interviewed for his job at Powderham, Tim Faulkner told Hugh Devon that he thought he would last three years, and his boss looked dismayed. 'But this place has a way of getting its hooks into you,' says Faulkner, now in his twelfth year.

'I couldn't just run a stately home. I need the challenge of big events, which is what I do now. It's showmanship. The feeling takes me back to the early days of running the regimental musical rides with thirty horses.'

Faulkner admits that there are plenty of unglamorous sides to his job, but that he can walk through a crowd of 20,000 people enjoying themselves and feel, 'It's not my performance, but I'm responsible for it.' When his twelve-year-old daughter Ginny was asked at school what her father did, she replied: 'My Daddy has parties and blows up balloons.'

In 1993, the Faulkners bought a house in nearby Mamhead, where the tourist roads give way to the old Devon lanes and the green landscape of forestry, grass and the distant sea. It should have been a place of tranquillity for them, away from their daily public duties at the castle.

But one day in 1998, that family world was to change for ever. Tim Faulkner told me the story as we sat in the Rose Garden at Powderham, talking until the warm sun of a summer's afternoon had long cooled into the cold sea breeze of evening.

'My wife Charlotte had brought our three-year-old son Ben to see me at work on a Saturday morning,' he recalled. 'I was working for an auction that was coming up. I didn't need to be working, and Ben was holding my hand and saying he wanted to stay with me. But I told Ben to go home with his mother and that I wouldn't be long. An hour later he drowned in our swimming pool.'

Faulkner, for all his military training and happy family life, admitted that the accident swept everything from under his feet. But the estate did not counsel: it acted. Lord Devon sent thirty men to the house and the swimming pool was gone in a day.

'I always feel sad when a young life dies – it is so unexpected,' Lord Devon told me days later when we were talking about Timothy. 'You see, I always knew Timothy, being so old, would go at some stage. It's the young lives I can't fathom.' He could have been thinking about Ben.

Faulkner himself quickly rallied. 'I wouldn't say I am a good Christian, but I wanted Ben to be buried in St Thomas's Church at Mamhead, but it had been closed for four months after the vicar punched a hole in the plasterwork, locked it up and declared it derelict and unfit for services.' So he went to see the Bishop of Exeter and asked for the church to be re-opened. Doing what he knows best, Tim said he and his wife Charlotte would raise the money. With a lot of help from the estate and the local villages, they raised £100,000.

'To me, it became a point of principle to get that church re-opened,' says Tim Faulkner. 'Ben was not sent into the world to rescue Mamhead church, but that's exactly what he did.'

The estate and the whole community supported this reaction. More than 400 people came to Ben's funeral and a marquee was put up by the lych gate. 'I did not ask for this,' says Tim Faulkner of his son's death. 'It was fate. But I am glad of it. Grief is like love.'

Today the church is open, and Tim Faulkner had asked me to go and look at it. I did, as the very last thing on the very last day of my visits to Powderham. There was the carriage sweep, the lych gate, and the churchyard which had stood there for 1,200 years.

A gentle evening mist hung about the tower and the night's dew was already on the grass. The place is remote but friendly and no one was around. Soon I came upon a small grave, bordered at its head and foot by rough-hewn Dartmoor granite.

In loving memory of
Benedict David Campbell

FAULKNER

Born 31st December 1994
Died 27th June 1998

I did not know why I had gone that evening or what day it was until I got home. It was 27 June. When he died Ben was almost the same age as I had been when I had first met Timothy. He was just too heavy for Superman to lift.

Eleven

The Devons

'Who else could have done this for you?' she whispered gloriously.

'No one in the world,' he answered her in a murmur of unconcealed despair.

Joseph Conrad, *Victory*

When Diana Watherston met Hugh Courtenay in the Scottish Borders in the summer of 1966, she was helping to run the Pony Club camp before planning to run away abroad, and he had just graduated from Magdalene College, Cambridge. 'He was painfully shy and wouldn't say a word,' she recalls. 'I was brought up to believe it was polite to talk to everyone and to make conversation.'

Nieces of the late Duchess of Roxburghe, Diana and her younger sister Rachel were imbued in the ways of Scottish Border country life and hunting with the Buccleuch foxhounds. This is the land of the Eildon Hills, and the writings of the Ettrick Shepherd. 'I'm totally a Border girl, a farmer's daughter, Scottish through and through,' says Diana Devon. 'My father was Master of the Buccleuch, my mother ran the Pony Club.'

But Diana was far from conventional. A teenage flourish of adding a second 'n' to her name – Dianna –

disappeared only when she became Countess of Devon.

The sisters were supposed to do the Season as debutantes but asked their parents if they could spend the money saved on a coming-out dance by travelling abroad. 'They were very understanding,' Rachel, then eighteen, told the *Sunday Express* at the time. 'They agreed that we would probably get much more out of seeing the world.' She continued: 'Doing the Season is a little played out, let's face it. A great deal of money goes on your party and what have you got at the end of it? Maybe you've made some good friends and maybe not.' Diana, a year older, had already travelled to Kenya and was planning to go to Australia.

Hugh Courtenay, at twenty-four, was 'filling in the summer' before starting in land and estate management. He had been invited to Scotland by Joe Scott Plummer, a friend from university.

Then came an invitation to Dublin Horse Show week, the height of the Irish social season. Balls were held each night in private houses and the heir to an English earldom with a castle that was still standing was a considerable catch. 'I had been invited by Joe Scott Plummer to Scotland and the Irish invitation only came later,' says Hugh Devon today. 'So naturally I stuck with the first invitation.'

Hugh and Diana's job at Pony Club camp was to collect two horses and ride them to the camp each morning – a job that was undertaken, against the dramatic landscape of the Border country, in one-sided silence.

'He was impossible to talk to,' Diana Devon says of Hugh. 'And here was me, this little girl, but that's where the romance started.'

Hugh's first invitation to Diana was the following spring to stay at Badminton for the Horse Trials with the Duke and Duchess of Beaufort. 'It was totally nerve-racking,' she recalls. 'Stuffed full of royals, including the Queen and Prince Philip. I think they were keeping their eye on Hugh for Princess Anne, but then he said could I come too?'

The next port of call was Powderham, with the late Lord and Lady Devon still very much in residence at the castle. 'I remember coming up the drive and actually being quite cross that Hugh hadn't warned me what Powderham was. I just thought it would be a country house,' says Diana Devon. 'Having just come from Badminton my new standards were set rather high. We arrived at the front door and this terribly nice man in a suit came out to say hello, and I assumed it was the butler. It was Hugh's father, so there followed something of a silence.'

But they got on very well together. 'He was a charming man, very intelligent with a marvellous mind, very much like his sister, Aunt Gabrielle. But I have to say, he was very lazy, and would much rather sit and read a newspaper than do anything.' So often, such behaviour is the result of war.

'He loved his shooting and had a tremendous knowledge of the estate,' continues Diana Devon. 'He could tell you where every drain was, every thorn bush.'

Diana marvelled at Christopher and Venetia Devon's living arrangements. 'When the castle opened in 1960, they skedaddled upstairs, I think to get away from the public. There was a door at the north end of the castle and then you climbed into a small lift and rattled your way upstairs to their private apartments. That always seemed a bit odd, because you were living in the country and couldn't just chuck the dog out.'

Not only do Hugh and Diana Devon live within strides of the Rose Garden so the dogs can alternate happily between the sofas and the lawn: for the last three years they have undertaken their own form of summer hibernation. They have a farmhouse on the estate near Kenn, in the middle of the fields, and in summer, they decamp there with the horses and the dogs.

'It takes a week to get packed up,' says Diana Devon. 'We leave the castle to earn its keep with the concerts.' This year, though, they have not gone to their hybernaculum because of Diana's duties as High Sheriff. 'It doesn't matter that there are always people outside the door,' she says. 'The only bad moment is if it's a lovely day and you just want to lie in the garden and take your clothes off.'

The day before we met, she had been 'shadowing' the Earl and Countess of Wessex. 'They flew in and had five appointments, at a very disabled children's home, the deaf

Hugh and Diana Devon in the grounds of Powderham Castle.

school, an old folk's home, Teignmouth hospital and another old folk's home. Amazing people. That's how they earn their keep.'

Diana Devon describes how the Queen still appoints high sheriffs by sticking a silver bodkin into a list of names. 'I don't know where she does it, maybe in her sitting room, but it all dates back to the time of Elizabeth I when she was in the garden doing her embroidery when the courtier from the Privy Council came in with the list.' As we speak, Diana Devon is herself embroidering.

It reminded me of a story that Lady Gabrielle Courtenay had told me just as I was leaving her at the Briary. 'I never mentioned, did I, about the time Timothy swallowed a gooseberry?' she said. 'My mother extracted it with a hat pin.'

Diana Devon remembers the Princess Royal, as Princess Anne, coming to stay at Powderham for the horse trials, which allowed Venetia Devon to practise all the skills she had so bravely tried to instil in the girls at the domestic science school. 'She was very keen to keep the standards up and appear frightfully grand. Princess Anne was longing just to be part and parcel of everything. Of course, she was nervous and could have a sharp tongue.'

'I found her super, though, I must say,' says Hugh Devon. 'We always got on very well together. She had to accept that she couldn't be as ordinary as she would have liked to have been.' She later lent them her wedding dress.

'I think her daughter is lucky in that way,' continues Hugh Devon about Zara Phillips. 'She's allowed to be ordinary. I think she's absolutely fantastic. Jolly attractive. Her mother was attractive too actually. She's awfully like her mother.'

Hugh Devon has inherited his father's prodigious memory. 'I can date my first memories of Powderham because my mother was going around doing the blackout during the war. I could not have been more than three. I can't date my first meeting with Timothy so easily because he had a calmer approach than the bombs.

'By the time I was compus, my father was back from the war, so his being away didn't make a lot of difference. Other people did, but we never had a special nanny. There was some game called "enders and devers" intended to keep the nanny up all night. Then a temporary nanny came and put a stop to all that. My mother asked her how she did it. "I will not have such things in my nursery," she replied.' At this moment Diana Devon helpfully produces a photograph that sits on a side table of her husband as a child and the admonishing nanny in a felt hat.

Of his mother, Diana Devon says: 'She was an incredibly forceful character. Hugh's father realised that it was much simpler really, if they were going to have a happy marriage, just to let her get on with her forcefulness, and that he would do things his way quietly.'

In 1974, it was pointed out to Venetia Devon that Macy's Store in New York was advertising some lingerie under the heading 'Lady Devon knows what you women want.' Apparently, they had been selling a range of 'Lady Devon's lingerie' for more than fifteen years.

Although sixty-five, Venetia Devon moved swiftly into action, suing the department store for a quarter of a million dollars. 'The right of my privacy has been violated,' she told the *Daily Mail*, adding, 'The money would certainly come in useful.' At the time, visitors to the castle were being charged forty pence a head.

The case, heard in the Philadelphia Federal Court, was unsuccessful. But Lady Devon, as befits the former Principal of the domestic science school, stood up for the rights of women to have control over their own virtue and underwear.

Venetia Devon with Timothy in 1987 outside the family chapel.

'The domestic science school was my mother's way of trying to do something to help the castle pay its way,' says Hugh Devon. 'I don't know how well it was thought through.'

Not yet in his teens, Hugh Devon did not really have much contact with the girls at the domestic science school. 'I think one of the very beautiful ones went off to become a famous high-class mistress. I never knew what her father did. One never wanted to ask.'

But he does recall the arrival of a South American beauty. 'You remember,' says Diana, prompting him, 'the Goldsmith Bird.' She, it turns out, was the South American tin heiress Isobel Patino, who was sent by her parents to Powderham to escape the attentions of James Goldsmith. 'Her father was trying to get her over Jimmy Goldsmith and make sure their relationship didn't work,' says Hugh. 'Then, of course, she died in childbirth, which was very sad. '

Hugh Devon had been very happy at Winchester and Cambridge. 'After that, I found a wife, really, and I haven't done too badly.'

The Devons have four children. When their eldest, Rebecca, was born, in 1969 (her second name is Eildon, after her mother's beloved Border hills), the bells were rung at Kenton Church, breaking a 400-year tradition that they should be pealed only for a male heir. It made up for Hugh's wartime loss when his mother had lamented: 'Poor little heir. No church bells. No fireworks.'

When their daughter Camilla married Captain Daniel Duff on 27 December 2003, the people putting up the marquee put a spike through the water main just outside the wisteria and Timothy's hibernation place. He had to be moved in a box of straw – echoing the movement of Gilbert White's tortoise when the beer house flooded at Selborne.

Like his father before him, Hugh Devon is a keen shot and there is a shoot at Powderham today. 'I can say that I think it's very good,' he says. 'It's not a big money-spinner – unless you treat things totally commercially, they never are. But it enables me to shoot here with my friends.'

Of his father's reluctance to open letters, Hugh Devon says: 'It was an unfortunate habit in a way. There were quite a lot of bills, but also there were quite a lot of cheques. It was quite effective, though. After a bit, no one ever wrote to him. They didn't bother and he didn't want to bother with it.'

What Hugh and Diana Devon did bother with was Timothy. 'He was in my psyche from the moment I arrived here,' says Diana Devon. 'Oddly enough, for me, he was one of the great responsibilities of inheritance here.

I mean he could die, whereas the castle wasn't exactly going to fall over. He had been such a huge character in Hugh and his family's life, that I found his presence quite anxious-making.'

When Diana Devon came to Powderham, Mallo, the old French governess, was still alive. Her duties were to look after Timothy and the dogs. She had a very strict routine. Timothy always got his lunch – usually strawberries – at two o'clock. Then the dogs would be taken for a walk. 'Such a routine was rather an old-fashioned way of doing things,' says Diana Devon.

'When it became our turn to look after Timothy, things had rather changed. Supper could happen at seven o'clock or ten o'clock, and I used to worry that I was letting Mallo down. Then I realised that Timothy could look after himself. There was really so much goodness in the grass, because we did not mow it, that he could cope very well. The only worry was whether he could hibernate in the winter, but he did this perfectly well by himself as well. Occasionally he tripped or fell upside down, but someone was never far away.'

Hugh Devon observes, 'The more feeding we encouraged him to do in the summer, the more glad he was to go into hibernation in the winter. That's the system, isn't it?'

The Devons learned to live with Timothy very happily. First thing in the morning, the alarm would be turned off, the shutters opened, the dogs would be let out and Timothy would be looked for. That was their routine.

Until about 1999, Timothy had never been to a vet. But there comes a time, even in the long life of a venerable chelonian, when the spring is no longer in one's step. The first worrying sign was raised by the Devons' daughter

Nell, when she rang them on their mobile while they were walking the course at the Badminton Horse Trials.

'Timothy's looking a bit dead, Mum,' she said.

'We came home and he was just sitting there looking floppy,' remembers Diana Devon.

Thus began the most intensive period of Timothy's care, worthy of a family that has produced so many nurses. 'I became nervous because as Hugh pointed out, he had never left the garden in our lifetime. But he was going slowly downhill and I had to take him to the vet in Exeter in a basket of Timothy grass, which we use to feed our horses.'

The St David's Veterinary Hospital in Exeter is well used to ancient and exotic animals. Throughout my life, I was charged with taking a succession of my father's Pekineses there for life-prolonging treatment. When they still looked after farm animals, I once took a ewe there, but was stopped by the police on the way. The sheep had jumped from the back to the front of the farm Deux Chevaux and was handling the central gearstick at the time of my apprehension. The policeman gave me a hand to get the sheep into the back again.

Timothy came under the charge of vet Jane Briars, in June 2002. 'He had pneumonia and jaundice and I kept him under supervision for a fortnight. Then he did very well and went home and put on weight.'

It was at this time that I saw Diana Devon in the distance at a large drinks party on the lawn of a Dartmoor farmhouse. She came running across to talk to me, and I imagined to say something very serious. 'Timothy has been unwell,' she said.

In April 2003, Timothy returned to Jane Briars. 'I would

sit out with him in the sun. He was a lovely patient, but a very independent soul. He became particular about what he ate.' This time Timothy had a sore left eye and needed help with eating. 'He was given a daily pinch of reptile food to go with his greens,' says Jane Briars, reading from Timothy's case notes.

Hugh and Diana also had to give Timothy injections, a time-consuming task, as it required waiting for him to release the arms of his claws from his shell. Hugh held him while Diana gave him his daily injection. 'He used to struggle on the floor a bit, but the injection boosted him up no end,' says Diana.

In February 2004, it was very hot and Timothy mistook the warm weather for spring. 'He was just cruising happily around the garden,' says Diana Devon. 'Then we went on holiday and I still find myself slightly blaming myself because he was left out in the middle of the garden and there were some very cold nights.'

'We put him back in his bedroom several times after that,' says Hugh Devon. 'Maybe we should have broken all the rules and brought him into the house in the end, but we didn't.'

Timothy died in the early days of spring, just as the first three shoots of the purple wisteria, under which he had lived for so long, had come out. Diana Devon took the sad journey back to the vet's to make sure. 'She was very upset,' says Jane Briars. 'But she knew in her heart he had died. Her first reaction was "How shall I tell Aunt Gabrielle?"'

'It may seem funny,' says Diana Devon. 'But every morning I used to say to myself, I wonder where Timothy is today? And he isn't there. Today I saw strawberries in the

Cash and Carry … It's like any bereavement.'

The last event to happen at Powderham in Timothy's lifetime was the engagement of Charles Courtenay, the Devons' 29-year-old son, to Alison Joy Langer. 'AJ', as she is known, was described by a newspaper as a 'stunning *Baywatch* television star,' having appeared on the popular television serial. It was suggested in the newspapers that the couple would marry next year at Powderham in a 'society' wedding. Either in the fine tradition of Diana Watherston's request to her parents that she should not have a coming-out ball or in respect of a period of mourning for Timothy, they married in private in a civil ceremony in California without telling anyone.

TWELVE

'To Sleep, Perchance to Dream': A family in mourning, a tortoise at rest

'Woe to the man whose heart has not learned while young to hope, to love – and to put its trust in life.'

Joseph Conrad, *Victory*

Timothy's life was on a grand scale, but his spirit was one of modesty. Even now it is difficult to comprehend the events which his great span of years encompassed.

Devon has changed out of all recognition since he first arrived to holiday at Powderham in a wicker basket in the 1920s, with a railway ticket and a thirst for azalea blossom. The city of Exeter has been rebuilt, but with none of its former civic majesty.

The cathedral, where Courtenay bishops and my own mitred forebear are remembered, is restored but now charges an entrance fee. Aeroplanes, which once Timothy only saw as bombers in the war, leave the local airport for anywhere in the world.

I hope that the world and Devon timelines which follow on pages 139 and 149, charting events that occurred during Timothy's life, will help to illustrate the uniqueness of his longevity. I hope they also recognise achievements perhaps not otherwise fully appreciated.

But in change there is constancy. At Powderham, after the visitors have left and the concerts have been played, the Rose Garden still lies peacefully as Timothy would have known it. 'We will never gather the wisteria leaves,' Diana Devon had told me. I know now what she means. Out on the estuary the boats still pass the churches with white spires of their own. The Devon red cliffs of Lympstone reflect their ancient past upon the water.

But, somehow, something has gone for ever, never to be replaced. The castle may not have fallen over, but something very personal to the family has quietly departed. The weight of responsibility may have gone, but a wistful memory and sadness have taken its place.

The word timothesis has been lodged with the *Oxford English Dictionary* as meaning 'wisdom in old age'. The dictionary editors require four more people to use this word before they submit it to their full panel for inclusion.

When I was in Oxford, making this request, I wrote down the name of the director as Penny Silver. But she is actually Penny Silva. Perhaps she is related to the Silvas of Itchen Abbas and therefore to the Courtenays? What she did tell me was that, although South African, she had English relatives who lived at Compton Castle in Devon who were called Walter Raleigh Gilbert. I was, there and then, able to produce an old press cutting from *The Times*, listing who had given dinner parties for Lady Katherine Watney's coming-out dance in 1958. On the list, among Fulfords, Rayners, Snows and other Devon notables, was Mrs Walter Raleigh Gilbert.

This is just one of several coincidences I experienced in writing the life of Timothy. When I talked to Christine Manning, she remembered how when she was a young girl my father's horse Claud had come to Powderham. 'Was yours the black German horse?' she said one day. Claud had been brought back from Austria by my father after the war and they had won the army show-jumping championships together. 'This horse is released from military service to return to the Devon home of Capt. Knight Bruce, on account of their special relationship,' read the faded telegram, which I still have, from his commanding officer.

Then there was my visit to Martin Roundell at the Elms, and seeing the graves of Corries of Shropshire at the Itchen Abbas church. In 1991, on a windy day, I had helped the stone carver, Belinda Eade, put up the headstone for Tom Corrie in a Shropshire churchyard.

As I was leaving Gilbert White's museum, where assistant Karen Bridgman had been so helpful, she told me she was going somewhere else. I asked where? 'To Painshill,' came her reply. I had worked on these Surrey gardens in 1987, with their follies and grottoes, when they had been forgotten for years by man and time alike.

At *The Spectator* summer party, I found myself signing my name in the visitors' book after that of the humorist Miles Kington. He had once written an article saying there should be a book about Timothy. We had never met before, yet there we were in the garden, among hundreds of people, talking about the tortoise. I was introduced to Kington by the writer John Michell, one of the great explicars of coincidence.

Then there was, of course, the sad but poignant

coincidence of visiting Benedict Faulkner's grave quite by chance on the anniversary of his death. If there is to be a word for wisdom in old age, let it now be timothesis.

My own first meeting with Timothy was as a four-year-old, when I was taken to Powderham by my father. The tortoise was the first thing that I saw, and I marvelled at his foreignness. Hugh Devon is right. There is something about those earliest memories which you never quite forget.

Lady Katherine Watney was my guide throughout this book, finding time to do so between caring for the church, running the Courtenay Society and looking after her sandy-coloured Labrador Piglet. Her only son, Michael Watney, has inherited the family's love of the country and looks after estates in Shropshire.

'Will we see you again?' she asked me towards the end. On the final day, as we stood in the rain in the car park, she asked me what I was doing next Thursday. The real answer was, and I started to say it, handing in the book. But halfway through saying it I saw her face and paused, then she said, 'Henley Regatta. Thursday. Antony and I used to go.' I could hardly have replied, 'Vespers.'

So the following Thursday I set off by train to the Rose and Crown in Henley. It was a typical June day, with sun and rain in equal measure. It was the England of Lady Katherine Watney, ordered, happy and optimistic. As the rowers went by, she explained in great detail the technicalities of the racing. How did she know all this, I asked. 'I used to put up the rowing teams and just listened to them over breakfast,' she replied.

I got to hear her singing when we both attended the Earl of Iddesleigh's funeral service in Exeter. By chance she was behind me and I heard her give an unmistakable lead.

In choosing my chapter headings, I have returned again and again to Joseph Conrad's *Victory*. Not only was he a writer without equal in his distillation of sea, sky and silence, but, as I have mentioned, he was orphaned to these shores and conquered them.

In the way that Gilbert White in his letter to Miss Hecky Mulso imagined what it might have been like to have been his tortoise, so, in some ways, Timothy had Conradian qualities.

I could have taken a more pastoral path, like Gilbert White, Kilvert or Cobbett. But none of them knew battleships and bombs.

In *Victory* Conrad's central character Axel Heyst imposes his own loneliness. He chooses to lose himself in the remote islands of the South China Seas. 'He was a strange being without needs,' writes Conrad.

Heyst does not love himself until he discovers the love of Lena, a chorus girl, who gives her life for him. For Heyst and Timothy love came only in discovery. And in their discovery was their redemption, as they were pulled from the ranks of abjection, be it from a ship's quarterdeck or an island hut.

Almost the last thing Lady Gabrielle Courtenay said to me about Timothy was this. 'I suppose I was fond of him, except that I didn't love him,' she said. 'You couldn't cuddle him, so it was a different kind of affection. But I would be furious if I thought anyone was going to hurt him.'

'I'm sorry that he's gone,' says Lady Gabrielle Courtenay of Timothy. 'He was a very peaceful sort of pet to have. It was very comforting to sit in the garden with him quietly munching around you.'

Timothy is buried under the purple wisteria in the Rose Garden where he spent much of the latter part of his life. It is there that he will be remembered by the family and many visitors to whom he was a light in a darkening world. This is his right and privilege. Mine has been to speak for a being, a beloved chelonian, who could not speak for himself.

World timeline

1844 *15 June* Lord Shaftesbury's Factory Act forbids the employment for more than twelve hours per day of women of all ages; their working week is limited to sixty-nine hours. Children as young as eight are permitted to work a maximum of six hours per day; there is to be compulsory education for children.

6 August The birth of Queen Victoria's second son, Alfred Ernest, at Windsor, is announced by telegraph. Within forty minutes, the news is printed and distributed in London by *The Times*.

23 October The future Poet Laureate, Robert Bridges, is born. Among others born in this year of 1844 are Karl Benz, automobile inventor; Gerard Manley Hopkins (28 July), poet; Friederich Wilhelm Nietsche, philosopher; Rimsky-Korsakov, composer; and Henry Rousseau, 'Le Douanier', fauvist artist.

J.M.W. Turner paints *Rain, Steam and Speed*, which is seized on as the spirit of the coming age.

The potato famine begins in Ireland. Millions will migrate.

1845 *1 May* Cricket is first played at the Oval in Kennington. Also this year is the first University Boat Race.

1848 *22 February* The Republican revolution breaks out in Paris. Later in the year, there are revolutions in Italy, Austria, Hungary and Germany.

10 April The Chartist plans for a mass rally and march to Parliament are crushed by the authorities. This radical British working-class movement, which calls for universal manhood suffrage, is suppressed by summary arrests over the rest of 1848. It will never rise again.

The Communist Manifesto, written by Karl Marx with his lifelong collaborator Friedrich Engels, is published.

1851 *1 May* Queen Victoria opens the Great Exhibition in Crystal Palace in Hyde Park.

1852 *18 November* The state funeral of the Duke of Wellington takes place.

1854 *28 March* The Crimean War begins. Britain and France declare war on Russia.

1857 *10 May* The Sepoy Mutiny in India begins at Meerut, from where the rebels march to Delhi and the mutiny spreads throughout the Ganges valley. The siege and surrender of Kanpur (Cawnpore) to Nana Sahib results in the massacre of British civilians on 15 July. Lucknow is under siege from 1 July to 25 September, when it is relieved by Havelock and Outram.

1858 *5 August* The first transatlantic cable is completed, and is opened by Queen Victoria and US President Robert Buchanan exchanging messages.

1859 *24 November* Charles Darwin's *On the Origin of Species by means of Natural Selection, or the Preservation of Favoured Races in the Struggle for Life*, is published.

1861 *4 March* Abraham Lincoln is inaugurated as sixteenth President of the United States.

1863 *10 January* The first section of the London Underground, the first in the world, is opened by W.E. Gladstone.

1865 *14–15 April* Abraham Lincoln is shot by John Wilkes Booth in the box of Ford's Theatre in Washington and dies the next morning.

18 December Slavery is abolished in the United States of America.

Joseph Lister pioneers antiseptic surgery by dressing wounds with carbolic acid.

1869 *16 November* The Suez Canal is formally opened.

1871 *18 January* The German Empire is proclaimed at Versailles at the conclusion of the Franco-Prussian War.

10 November Henry Morton Stanley meets Dr David Livingstone in the African village of Ujiji on the shores of Lake

Tanganyika. Stanley utters the famously stiff greeting, 'Dr Livingstone, I presume?'

1874 *15 April* The first Impressionist exhibition is held in Paris: 165 pictures by thirty-three artists, including Monet, Renoir, Degas, Sisley, Cézanne and Pissaro, are on show. Curious crowds come to view, but no pictures are bought. Although ridiculed at the time, it marks the beginning of all modern art movements.

1876 *7 March* Alexander Graham Bell patents his invention of the telephone.

26 June At the Battle of Little Big Horn in Montana, Sitting Bull and his Sioux massacre General Amstrong Custer and his men.

1877 Thomas Alva Edison invents the phonograph.

1879 Thomas Alva Edison develops the incandescent electric light.

1887 *21 June* Queen Victoria's Golden Jubilee is celebrated throughout Britain.

1888 *31 August – 9 November* Jack the Ripper, probably the most notorious murderer, kills five victims in the East End of London. He or she has never been positively identified. The heir presumptive to the throne, the Duke of Clarence, and the artist Sickert, are among numerous suspects.

1889 The Eiffel Tower in Paris is completed. Named after its designer, French engineer Gustave Eiffel, it was begun in 1887, and is completed in time for the Paris Exhibition. Built of iron, it stands 984½ feet high.

1894 *21 May* The Manchester Ship Canal, begun in 1887, is opened.

1899 *12 October* The Anglo-Boer War begins when the Boer demand that British troops withdraw is refused. Mafeking and Kimberley are besieged.

1901 *22 January* Queen Victoria dies at Osborne, Isle of Wight. She was born on 24 May 1819 and reigned for sixty-four years. She lived through the growth of British industry and the Empire and saw her children married into seven of Europe's royal families. She is succeeded by Edward VII.

1903 *17 December* Wilbur and Orville Wright launch the first heavier-than-air flying machine at Kitty Hawk, North Carolina. Four flights are made, with the longest travelling nearly 850 feet in almost one minute.

1904 Harry Houdini (born Ehrich Weiss in Budapest on 24 March 1874) returns to London. He escapes from 'supercuffs' in a challenge from the *London Mirror*.

1906 *8 May* Emmeline Pankhurst and the Suffragettes begin a militant campaign for voting rights.

1910 *6 May* Edward VII dies and is succeeded by George V.

20 August The funeral service for Florence Nightingale is held in St Paul's Cathedral. The heroine reformer of Scutari Hospital in the Crimean War is then buried in the churchyard of East Wellow in Hampshire.

1912 *18 January* Captain Robert Falcon Scott and his party reach the South Pole, having been beaten to it by Roald Amundsen, who reached it on 16 December 1911.

15 April The largest ship of her day, and supposedly unsinkable, SS *Titanic* sinks after striking an iceberg on her maiden voyage from Southampton to New York. More than 1,500 of the 2,340 passengers and crew are drowned.

1914 *4 August* Great Britain declares war on Germany.

1915 *25 April* British and French forces land at Gallipoli. The aim is to force the Turkish held Dardanelles, and join up with Russia. The campaign incurs huge losses on both sides. The allies finally withdraw in January 1916. Gallipoli is especially associated with the heroism and sacrifices of the Australian and New Zealand contingents.

1918 *16 July* The former Tsar of Russia, Nicholas II, and his family are executed by Bolsheviks in a cellar in Ekaterinburg in the Urals. Their deaths mark the irrevocable move to Communism in Russia.

1921 *16 December* Parliament ratifies the Irish agreement, opening the way to the establishment of the Irish Free State in 1922.

1924 *3 August* Joseph Conrad, the eminent author, dies at Bishopsbourne, near Canterbury, in Kent.

1926 *27 January* John Logie Baird transmits the first television images in a demonstration held at the Royal Institution in London.

1928 *30 September* Professor Alexander Fleming, of St Mary's Hospital in London, announces his discovery of penicillin.

All women in Britain over the age of twenty-one are given the same voting rights as men.

1936 *20 January* George V dies. He is succeeded by Edward VIII.

11 December Edward VIII abdicates. He gives up the throne for the American divorcee Mrs Wallis Simpson, 'the woman I love'.

1937 *12 May* Prince Albert Frederick Arthur George, Duke of York, is crowned King George VI at Westminster Abbey. His consort is Queen Elizabeth, née Elizabeth Bowes-Lyon, daughter of the Earl of Strathmore.

Pablo Picasso paints one of his masterpieces, *Guernica*, a mural evoking the bombing raid carried out in the Spanish Civil War.

1938 *14 January* Walt Disney's *Snow White and the Seven Dwarfs* is shown in New York.

30 September The Prime Minister, Neville Chamberlain, returns from his Munich meeting with Adolf Hitler. He promises 'peace in our time'.

1939 *3 September* Great Britain declares war on Germany.

1940 *10 May* Neville Chamberlain resigns as Prime Minister of Britain and is suceeded by Winston Churchill.

1945 *8 May* Britain takes to the streets to celebrate the end of the war in Europe.

6 August An atomic bomb, of explosive power equal to a 'nominal' 20,000 tons, is dropped on Hiroshima. Another, dropped on Nagasaki three days later, convinces Japan to surrender. The Second World War is over.

1947 *January–March* Snow falls every day somewhere in Britain. The weather has been cruelly deceptive, with mild temperatures in some places up to eleven degrees centigrade in mid-January. Then, on 23 January, the blizzard begins in the south-west. Many villages in Devon are isolated under the heaviest snowfall since 1891. Thaw floods then bring widespread misery to post-war austerity Britain.

1948 *30 January* Mahatma Gandhi is assassinated by a Hindu nationalist.

14 May The new state of Israel is proclaimed.

1951 The first Miss World Beauty Competition is held. London-based, it now claims to be the oldest and largest beauty pageant in the world.

1952 *6 February* George VI dies, and is succeeded by Elizabeth II.

24 November Agatha Christie's play *The Mousetrap* opens at the Ambassador's Theatre in London. It will become the world's longest continually running play.

1953 *29 May* Sir Edmund Hillary of New Zealand and Sherpa Tensing Norgay of Nepal reach the summit of the highest mountain in the world, Mount Everest.

1954 *6 May* Roger Bannister, a 25-year-old medical student, runs a mile in under four minutes at the university track at Iffley Road, Oxford. More than 1000 runners have now broken the four-minute mile.

1955 *30 September* James Dean, actor and teen hero, is killed in a road smash outside Los Angeles.

1960 *21 March* Fifty-six black Africans are killed and 162 injured as police open fire on pass-law demonstrators at Sharpeville Police Station, South Africa.

The Charles Darwin Research Centre is established by an

International Committee in order to promote research, conservation and education in the Galapagos Islands. Its logo trademark is a tortoise. The centre is located on Isla Santa Cruz and has tortoise rearing and adult tortoise houses. A famous inhabitant of the centre is 'Lonesome' George. He is the last turtle of the sub-species *geochelone elephantopus abingdoni*. Estimates of his age vary. Scientists are trying to find him a mate.

1961 *20 August* The East Germans begin to erect the Berlin Wall, separating the eastern and western sectors of the city.

1963 *27 March* The British Railways Board report is published. Under the chairmanship of Dr Beeching, the Board proposes closing 2,128 stations, cutting the railway network by a quarter, scrapping 8,000 coaches and 67,700 jobs.

1963 *28 August* Martin Luther King gives his 'I have a dream' speech at a civil rights demonstration in Washington.

November 22 President John F. Kennedy is assassinated in Dallas, Texas; Lee Harvey Oswald, a pro-Castro activist, is arrested.

1965 *15 August* The Beatles begin a North American tour at Shea Stadium, New York. They sing their classics, including 'Twist and Shout', 'Hard Day's Night', and 'I Feel Fine'. Playing to 55,000 hysterical fans, it is seen as the world's first stadium rock concert.

1966 *30 July* England wins the World Cup in football for the first time. Under manager Alf Ramsey and captain Bobby Moore, the team defeats West Germany at Wembley by four goals to two.

21 October In the Aberfan disaster, 116 children and twenty-eight adults are killed when coal slag-heap engulfs a school near Merthyr Tydfil.

1967 *8 May* Sir Francis Chichester sails into Plymouth and a tumultuous welcome after his epic 28,500-mile lone yacht voyage around the world.

December The first microwave ovens appear on the market.

1968 *4 April* US civil rights leader Dr Martin Luther King is assassinated in Memphis Tennessee. He was born on 15 January 1929.

6 November Richard Nixon is elected President of the United States.

1969 *21 July* Man sets foot on the moon for the first time.

1974 *14 September* Chia Chia, the giant panda, arrives at London Zoo with his mate, Ching Ching. They are goodwill gifts from the government of China to Prime Minister Edward Heath, who visits the pair there. In 1988, Chia Chia will move to Mexico City as a mate for Tohui. He will die at the age of nineteen.

1975 *31 April* Saigon in South Vietnam falls, marking the end of fifteen years of the United States' involvement in the Vietnam War.

The Hawksbill tortoise is declared an endangered species. It is the sea tortoise most used for tortoiseshell toiletry products, popular with the wealthy since the eighteenth century. Trading in tortoiseshell is also declared illegal. Declarations made after 1975, and subscribed to by major users such as Japan, do not halt the decline of sea tortoises.

1976 *January* Concorde, the world's only supersonic passenger aircraft, goes into service with flights to Bahrain and Rio de Janeiro.

1979 *4 May* Margaret Thatcher becomes Britain's first woman Prime Minister.

1981 *29 July* Lady Diana Frances Spencer, aged twenty, marries Charles, Prince of Wales.

1981 *20 December* Eight crewmen of the Cornish *Penlee* lifeboat are drowned while attempting to save passengers from a coaster. Four passengers, taken on board in the hurricane-lashed sea, die on the rocks. Four other passengers are lost. All the lifeboatmen were from the small harbour of Mousehole.

1982 *2 April* Argentina invades the Falkland islands and a Royal

Navy Task Force is despatched on 5 April from Portsmouth. The islands are recaptured when the Argentinians surrender on 14 June.

1987 *16 October* The south-east of England is hit by the worst storm since 1703: 16 million trees are felled, and 16 people die. The weatherman, Michael Fish, is furiously criticised for saying, 'A lady has rung in to ask if there is going to be a hurricane tonight ... there is not!' He is technically right: it is not *quite* a hurricane. He is forgiven, and remains a weatherman.

1989 *10 November* The Berlin Wall begins to be dismantled by East and West Germans at the stroke of midnight. It marks the collapse of the Eastern bloc, controlled by Soviet Russia, termed by Ronald Reagan 'the evil empire'.

1990 *11 February* After more than twenty-five years in captivity, Nelson Mandela is released from Pollsmoor Prison near Cape Town. His release marks the beginning of the end for apartheid in South Africa, and heralds the holding of democratic elections.

1996 *5 July* Dolly the Sheep, the first mammal to be successfully cloned from an adult cell, is born.

1996 *8 August* Their Royal Highnesses the Prince and Princess of Wales are formally divorced at the High Court in London.

1997 *2 May* The Labour Party in Britain wins a landslide election victory. Tony Blair becomes the new Prime Minister.

1997 *7 May* Jeanne Calment dies in a nursing home in Arles, France. She was 122 years old, and the oldest person ever to have had her age verified by official documents. She rode a bicycle until she was 100, and gave up smoking at the age of 116 because someone told her it was bad for her health. She remembered serving Vincent van Gogh at the shop where she worked.

31 August Diana, Princess of Wales and Dodi Fayed are killed in a car crash in Paris

1997 *5 September* Mother Teresa dies in her Missionaries of Charity Home in Calcutta.

1999 *31 December* As the sun sets on the twentieth century, the first of a nationwide chain of beacons is lit on Unst, the most northerly of the Shetland Islands.

2000 *June* The US Human Genome project announces the completion of a working draft of the entire human genome sequence. The project has identified all 30,000 genes in human DNA. Man has turned from mapping planet earth to mapping himself.

2001 *20 January* President George W. Bush is inaugurated as forty-third President of the United States.

2001 *11 September* The attack on the World Trade Center in New York takes place. An estimated 3,000 deaths occur when four US airliners, hijacked by Islamic extremists, crash into the twin towers of the World Trade Center in New York, the Pentagon in Washington, DC, and a field in Pennsylvania. The exact number of deaths will never be known.

2002 *30 March* Queen Elizabeth the Queen Mother dies peacefully in her sleep, at the age of 101, at Royal Lodge in the grounds of Windsor Castle.

2002 *23 September* The Countryside March on London takes place. An official 407,791 attend, with an estimated 70,000 coming from the West Country. It is a protest against central government neglect of the shires and an assertion of countryside identity.

2003 *20 March* Coalition forces, led by the United States with British participation, invade Iraq. By 15 April, President Saddam Hussein and his government are overturned. Iraq is still occupied in 2004 as the coalition struggles to install viable government.

2004 *11 March* Ten bombs explode on rush-hour commuter trains in Madrid: 190 people are killed, and more than 1,400 are injured. It is the worst peacetime attack in modern Spanish history. Blamed on Islamic extremists, the outrage influences the election defeat of the conservative Popular Party, which supported the coalition invasion of Iraq.

Devon timeline

1844 *March–November* At least six ships are wrecked off the Devon coast this year. In March, the *Fortune* is lost at Broad Sands with the loss of ten crewmen. In September, *Friends* is lost off Ilfracombe; then, within a fortnight, *The Little Family* is wrecked off Torbay and three of her crew are lost. The *David* and the *Knysna* are driven ashore at Bude in the first half of November, but fortunately the crews are saved. Soon afterwards, the *Fairy Queen* is lost at Saunton Sands, Braunton. Her crew is also saved.

1 May The opening of the Bristol and Exeter Railway takes place 'in a manner worthy the completion of so Important an undertaking'. The first train, from London, steams into Exeter St David's station.

1845 *17 June* The Exeter Express train from Paddington has an accident near Slough. One of the passengers is Mrs Amy Davy of Honiton, lacemaker to the Queen.

10 October The world fails to come to an end, despite the predictions of two visionaries in Tiverton.

1845–7 Charles Fowler undertakes major renovation of Powderham Castle for William Courtenay, 10th Earl of Devon. It includes a large, single-storey dining hall, but this is not fitted up until 1860.

1849 *11 January* *Trewman's Exeter Flying Post* reports that five ships, carrying over a thousand emigrants, are preparing to sail from Devon to Australia. It is part of the mass exodus from the county during the nineteenth century, caused by high unemployment and poor living conditions.

1851 *13 June* Queen Victoria holds a costume ball. Many men at the ball are shown with lace on their breeches. Years later, the husband of an old Honiton lacemaker claims that his wife had made a pair of lace breeches over satin for Prince Albert. Perhaps it was for this occasion. It was a far more modest order than that for Queen Victoria's wedding dress, which was composed entirely of Honiton lace. It was made at Beer. The order was given to Jane Bidney, who chose 100 of the best lacemakers for the task. The dress cost £1,000. The pattern was destroyed immediately afterwards.

1854 *9 January* Riots, in protest at the high price of bread, take place in Exeter. The mob, most of whom are women and children, attack bakeries and shops in the city. The disorder reflects the depressed state of Devon in the nineteenth century.

1855 *1 January* The School of Art opens in Exeter. It is a 'distant ancestor' of the University of Exeter. It offers day and evening tuition in its premises over the Lower Market in Milk Street. Classes for ladies are held during the day. The fee is one, or one and a half, guineas. 'Industrial Classes' of people may attend in the evenings after work, and they pay two shillings per month for tuition. The School of Art soon becomes a flourishing institution.

9 February There are reports of mysterious prints in the snow in Devon. A two-legged, hoofed creature appears to walk 100 miles across walls, rooftops and fields.

1860 *18 July* The London–Yeovil–Exeter line opens with the arrival of the first train into Exeter. The day is a general holiday in the city, with a great banquet at Northernhay attended by 500 people.

1861 An old and once important medieval building to the south-east of Powderham Castle is converted into a chapel.

1862 *30 August* Robert Davy of Countess Wear, Topsham dies at the age of 99 years and 10 months. He built many ships on the River Exe 'for his Majesty's service and private trade'. One was *Terror*, a bomb-ketch, built in 1813 and later used for polar exploration. In 1845, the vessel was fitted with auxiliary steam power for Sir John Franklin's fateful expedition in search of the North-West Passage, from which no one returned. The *Terror* and the *Erebus* were eventually abandoned in the ice on 22 April 1848.

1866 *3 March* 200 special constables, 131 constabulary, and 150 soldiers are sent to Devon Great Consols Mine near Tavistock.

Rioting is expected from the miners, who have formed an association with the other miners of Devon and Cornwall. The management objects to one of the proposed rules of the society, and has been alarmed at receiving coffins of clay inscribed 'died 1866'. The mine chairman, however, addresses the miners, who point out that they have not yet adopted the rule. All goes off peacefully, and the press applauds the triumph of good British sense.

1869 *Lorna Doone* is published. The author, R.D. Blackmore, was educated at Blundell's School, Tiverton. This historical adventure novel is forever linked with Devon and Exmoor in the mind of the English-speaking world. Many years hence, in 1906, male students at Yale University will vote it as their favourite novel.

1882 *28 October* A French Benedictine community, exiled from France, arrives to establish modern Buckfast Abbey. It is the genesis of the twenty-first century's thriving community on the banks of the River Dart near Buckfastleigh. Arguably, it represents the greatest monastic comeback in Devon since the Dissolution of the Monastries in 1538.

The Eddystone Lighthouse, built by Sir James Douglass, is lit.

1883 *3 May* Reverend John Russell, the hunting parson, dies in his eighty-eighth year at Black Torrington. He is buried at Swimbridge.

1887 *21 June* The Golden Jubilee of the reign of Queen Victoria is celebrated throughout Britain. In Exeter, 'from early morning until late at night there was an endless round of entertainments and interesting ceremonies', according to *The Evening Post*, Exeter.

5 September Disaster strikes on the first night of the *Romany Rye* at Exeter's Theatre Royal, built in 1886. A gas lamp sets fire to scenery on the stage. In the panic, people are trapped between the flames and the mass audience trying to escape. Only two people escape alive from the gallery. As the fire consumes the theatre some 160 people lose their lives. 'Such were the horrible circumstances of the tragedy that the exact number of victims could not be ascertained.'

1890 *15 September* Agatha Christie is born at Torquay.

1891 *March* Unseasonal gale-force winds and blizzards sweep southern England. In Devon, wrecks litter the coast, and railways and roads are snowed up. Thousands of cattle and ponies are frozen to death, and the bird life is decimated. A train on Dartmoor is completely covered in snow.

1904 *1 January* The first registration of cars in Exeter records twelve motor vehicles in the city.

1905 *4 April* The first of the electric trams, replacing the horse-drawn trams introduced in 1880, is brought into service in Exeter.

1906 *30 May* At about twelve minutes past two in the morning, HMS *Montagu* is grounded on the treacherous Shutter Rock at the south-west corner of Lundy Island. In dense fog, a strong prevailing current has driven the vessel off course. Launched at Devonport in 1901, she is 'one of the most recently commissioned battleships and pride of the Channel Fleet'. The court martial opens on 15 August 1906 to try Captain T.B.S. Adair and the navigating officer, Lieutenant Dathan. They are found guilty of stranding or losing HMS *Montagu*.

1910–30 Sir Edwin Lutyens builds Castle Drogo at Dewsteignton for the tea merchant, and founder of the Home and Colonial Stores, Julius Drewe. It is Lutyens' major work in Devon. Gertrude Jekyll advises on natural planting for the long approach drive.

1911 *June–July* The Duke of Bedford sells large estates in Devon, particularly around Tavistock. It is the start of the selling-up of great Devon estates, which is to continue through the twentieth century.

27 July 'Colonel' Cody lands at Whipton in the *Daily Mail* 1,010-mile air race over England and Scotland for a £10,000 prize. The race is won by Lieutenant Conneau of the French navy. This is the race featured in the film *Those Magnificent Men in their Flying Machines*, which will be made some half a century later.

1918 *May* The Devonshire Regiment loses 518 out of 550 men at

Bois de Buttes while stemming the last German push. The entire regiment is awarded the Croix de Guerre by the French government.

14 December Devon women – those aged at least thirty – vote for the first time.

1919 *28 November* American-born Viscountess Nancy Astor becomes Britain's first woman MP. She wins the safe Tory seat of Plymouth.

1924 *2 January* Sabine Baring-Gould dies at the age of ninety. Parson of Lew Trenchard, hymn-writer, novelist and antiquarian, he wrote 'Onward Christian Soldiers'.

1925 Martin Coles Harman buys Lundy Island, which lies eleven miles off the coast of North Devon. Only three miles long and half a mile wide, it has long had the mythical status of being 'independent'. Harman prints Lundy stamps, issues Lundy coins and flies the flag of his 'self-governing dominion'. He loses a court case about Lundy's status in 1931.

1926 *9 May* In the midst of the General Strike, an angry Plymouth crowd, reported to be 15,000 strong, gathers to see whether the trams are working, and is attacked with batons by plainclothes and uniformed police officers.

1927 Henry Williamson's *Tarka the Otter* is published. It is awarded the Hawthornden Prize. Williamson wrote it during the many years he lived in Georgeham, North Devon, before the Second World War. In future years, the railway from Exeter to Barnstaple will be known as 'the Tarka Line'.

1932 *14 July* The unique Exhibition of Early Devon Painters at the Royal Albert Memorial Museum is opened by Lord Conway of Allington at two-thirty in the afternoon. It includes works by Nicholas Hilliard, Richard Crosse, Richard Cosway, Francis Towne, Joshua Reynolds, his pupil James Northcote, Benjamin Robert Haydon, John Gendall, William Traies, his son Frank Downman Traies, and others.

1937 *12 May* The Earl of Devon is one of the minor peers attending the Coronation of George VI. In Devon, the first commercial flight into Exeter airport takes place. A Leopard Moth of Air Dispatch lands with photographs of the Coronation for the *Express & Echo*.

31 May Exeter airport is fully opened for use.

13 July The Earl of Devon celebrates his twenty-first birthday. A party and ball are held at Powderham Castle.

15 November The Earl of Devon has sold off more of his estates, this time in Alphington and Dawlish.

1938 *8 October* Among a number of titled people in the record divorce list for the Michaelmas law term – which begins next Wednesday – is the Earl of Cottenham's petition for the dissolution of his marriage to the Countess of Cottenham. It is undefended. The Earl of Devon, aged twenty-two, is cited as co-respondent. He succeeded to his title in 1935.

1941 *20 March* At around nine o'clock in the evening, the Luftwaffe begins to bomb Plymouth. Over the next few months, many hundreds are killed and thousands of buildings are destroyed.

1942 *1 March* HMS *Exeter* is 'scuttled by her own crew after heroic action against overwhelming Japanese forces in the Dutch East Indies'. Fifty-four officers and men are lost during the action. Many more will die as prisoners-of-war in Japanese hands. Built at Devonport, HMS *Exeter* was launched on 18 July 1929. In December 1939 she was at the Battle of the River Plate when the German pocket-battleship *Admiral Graf Spee* was destroyed.

23 April–4 May There are four air raids on Exeter, all in the early hours of the morning of 23 April. A total of 242 people are killed and 582 injured. The greatest damage occurs on 4 May. It lasts from 1.36 a.m. until 2.50 a.m., with widespread destruction to the city centre. Code-named after the German tourist guidebook, these 'Baedecker' raids are part of the attacks ordered by Hitler on historic English towns in retaliation for the bombing of Lubeck.

1942 *4 May* German radio broadcasts that 'Exeter was the jewel of the west ... We have destroyed that jewel, and the Luftwaffe will return to finish the job.'

1944 Evelyn Waugh writes at least part of *Brideshead Revisited* at Easton Court on Dartmoor, near Chagford.

1952 *16 August* Thirty-six people are dead and thousands made homeless when rivers burst their banks at Lynmouth, North Devon.

1958 *August* Speedclimbing is introduced at Wiscombe Park, seat of the Chichesters, near Honiton. It still continues today.

1962–3 *December–January* Heavy snowfalls in Devon and the rest of England cause traffic chaos and the widespread death of cattle and ponies. People wonder if it is 'the worst winter ever'. It is indeed the coldest winter for 223 years. With snowdrifts up to twenty feet deep, people are trapped in their homes, villages are cut off, power lines go down, and trains are cancelled.

1966 *11 July* The Exeter County Ground stadium is the scene of England's victory over Russia in the 1966 Speedway series. The home team, with two Exeter riders, now has an unassailable three-to-one lead. It avenges the record-breaking Russian triumph of 1965, in the same stadium, when the team's leader, Plechanov, broke the track record.

1966 *30 July* The Kinks, currently 'top of the pops' with 'Sunny Afternoon', give a concert in a field at Pinhoe, near Exeter. They arrive two hours late, at a quarter to midnight, and play for ten minutes. Six thousand disappointed West Country fans are infuriated. The group claims to have miscalculated the travel time. History, however, wonders. It is the day that England won the football World Cup…

1977 The M5 motorway reaches Exeter.

1998 *29 October* The Poet Laureate, Ted Hughes, dies at the age of sixty-eight. For many years, he had lived in North Tawton, Devon. After his famously tragic married life with the American poet Sylvia Plath, he married his second wife, Carol. His Devon life is recorded in his *Moortown Diaries*.

2000 *31 December* The worst floods in living memory hit the Axe Valley in East Devon. A tidal wave sweeps across the fields, inundating homes around Axminster. It is attributed to the wettest autumn on record and water running off frozen ground. Pointing to climate change, it is a pattern repeating all over Devon.

2001 *February* An outbreak of foot-and-mouth disease is confirmed in Britain, leading to the culling of millions of head of stock. It is unwittingly introduced to Devon by a sheep dealer who bought animals in the north of England.

April Phoenix, a white calf found beside its dead mother on a farm in Membury, is spared the foot-and-mouth cull after a public outcry. Three weeks later, she is signed up to appear in a London pantomime.

November Devon is declared foot-and-mouth free.

2002 *6 August* The eccentric West Country artist Robert Lenkiewicz dies in Plymouth. He is notorious for embalming and keeping the body of a tramp friend. After his death, his paintings sell well.

30 December Mary Wesley dies in her secluded cottage in Totnes, aged ninety. Famously publishing her first novel at the age of seventy, she went on to write her best-known book, *The Camomile Lawn*, in 1984.

2003 *19 May* The polar guide Pen Hadow, aged forty-one and from Hexworthy, makes history by reaching the North Geographic Pole from Canada. He is the first person to reach it alone and without being resupplied. As he waits to be evacuated, the strain is telling. He sends a message to *The Times* on 23 May: 'I'm going loony and deeply weird.'

1 July Members of Parliament vote for a ban on all forms of hunting by 362 to 208 votes. It amends the Hunting Bill into a total ban on all fox, deer and hare hunting.

1 November Thousands of hunters gather at Honiton showground to vow they will break the law if hunting is banned.

13 November The Planning Inspector gives the go-ahead for the building of new towns near Broadclyst and at Sherford in the South Hams. The building of 3,000 and 4,000 new homes respectively is greeted with dismay by protesters. It signals major changes ahead in the county.

Acknowledgements

The Gilbert White Museum, Selborne, Hampshire. Telephone: 01420 511 275. Open 11.00 a.m. to 5.00 p.m. from 1 January to 24 December.

Powderham Castle, Kenton, Devon. Telephone: 01626 890 243. www. powderham.co.uk. Open 11.00 a.m. to 5.00 p.m from April to September.

The Natural History Museum, London. Telephone: 0207 942 5000. www.nhm.ac.uk. Open Monday to Saturday 10.00 a.m. (11.00 a.m. Sunday) to 5.50 p.m.

The National Maritime Museum, Greenwich, London. Telephone: 0208 858 4422. www.nmm.ac.uk. Open 10.00 a.m. to 6.00 p.m. (5.00 p.m. in winter).

The Florence Nightingale Museum, St Thomas's Hospital, London. Telephone: 0207 620 0374. www. florence-nightingale.co.uk. Open 10.00 a.m. to 4.30 p.m.

West Country Studies Library, Exeter, Devon. Telephone: 01392 384 216. www.devon.gov.uk/library/locstudy. Open Monday to Saturday from 9.30 a.m.

In addition to those people acknowledged in the text, I would like to thank the following, who have been of especial assistance in the writing of this book: Felicity Harper, archivist; Powderham Castle; Roddy Martine; Colin and O-Lan Style; Laura Snook; *Western Morning News*; Tim Stanley-Clarke; Peter Waite; West Country Studies Library; *Private Eye*; The Powderham Estate for the many photographs they supplied; and also the Solent News and Photo Agency.

Index

Index